The Mothers of Change

By Anastacia J. Nutt

R.J. Stewart
Books

The Mothers of Change
By Anastacia J Nutt

Published by:

R J Stewart Books
PO Box 58
Dexter OR 97431
www.rjstewart.net

Printed in the United States of America and in The United Kingdom

A Catalogue record for this book is available from the Library of Congress.

ISBN: 978-0-9819246-8-7

The Mother Prayer

By Anastacia Nutt, 2009

In your name, Ama
Dark Mother, Divine Mother,
She who dwells within the depths of Creation,
Weaving her gifts of destruction, purification and regeneration,

Help us to receive them,
And to live a just life,
That we may be drawn down into you again in peace.

In your name, Aima
Bright Mother, Divine Mother,
She who dwells in the heights of Creation
Showering down her gifts of love, mercy and compassion,

Help us to receive them,
And to live a just life,
That we may be uplifted into you again in peace.

Ama

Aima

Omen

The Mothers of Change

Introduction

My pilgrimage to the heart of the Divine Feminine began in 1997 when I embarked upon a two year sojourn, walking with twenty-two different Mother Goddesses in succession, one after another. It is an understatement to say that this journey changed the course of my life. What was initiated then inspired me to co-lead the Women's New Moon and The Path of the Ceremonial Arts programs; this too bore fruit beyond its initial garden as the American/Israeli/Arab Women of Vision program waxed and waned.

The deep understanding nurtured within me during this important twelve year cycle, culminates in the prayer that begins this book, written two years ago, at the commencement of my work with *The Mothers of Change*. Its recitation rekindles the remembrance of all we truly are: physical manifestations of the Divine powers of Creation, bequeathed from above and below, always and forever.

The prayer begins in reverence to Ama, the Qabalists' Dark Mother Goddess. She is Orchil, the Weaver Goddess of the Underworld who we visit first in our work with *The Mothers of Change*; for it is she who gifts us with the physical matter of our existence, and she who collects the same back unto herself upon our death. The prayer then pays respect to Aima, the Qabalists' Bright Mother Goddess. She is Anankê, the Weaver Goddess of the Overworld who we visit last in our work with *The Mothers*; for it is she who gifts us with our natal characteristics according to the necessity of our soul's purpose. And when our life is complete, she gathers us into her celestial home where we await the future life to come.

Working alongside and within the greater embrace of these two Weaver Mothers of the Over and Underworlds are the temporal Mothers who mediate the spiritual powers of the Four-Fold Nature of Creation. In the worldly pantheons they are known by many different names. However varied their cultural expressions, their spiritual purpose unites them in a singular intent: to mediate the transformational, spiritual powers of Air/East, Fire/South, Water/West and Earth/North to humanity, according to our individual and collective needs. Though there are many worldly temporal Goddesses, it was the Mothers of the Western Mysteries who directly inspired this new work. Thus Athena, Sekhmet, Miryam and Inanna complement our purpose and complete the Divine sextet.

The Mothers of Change are the Divine Feminine forces who, over the course of our lives, guide and direct our course with the same balance of love and discipline as our human guardians. When we work them in this unique sacromagical manner, these six Mothers enable us to face and gracefully navigate the forces of change challenging humanity and the planet today.

Without a doubt, we are facing unprecedented change at this time; no one denies this social, spiritual, political and environmental truth. However, those who would make us believe that these forces of change must be "battled," "conquered" and "commanded" are offering neither wisdom nor truth. Those who fill our minds with the fears of externally-derived tyrannies, be they human, geologic, viral or technological, to which our only response is an embattled one, are offering neither wisdom nor truth. These two precious gifts can never be found in the throes of separation; but only within the Grace of the unity consciousness of all living beings. To this end, we must all strive as the spiritual human ambassadors of the human race.

Various sources tell us that the 21st century was destined to be a time of great change. The discovery that awaits us is how best to live within these times while continuing to offer ourselves to the world. *The Mothers of Change* help us adjust to the changing Cosmos, while staying fully engaged and awake. So, as the prayer declares, we may live a just life; and when we die, we may be simultaneously drawn down and uplifted into them again, in peace.

~ Anastacia J. Nutt
Spring Equinox 2011

Establishing Common Ground

Before delving into the methods associated with *The Mothers of Change* work, we must first establish our spiritual and cultural common ground; for without this, the flourishing of our esoteric work cannot be assured. Thus, let us begin by defining the ubiquitous terms "Goddess" and "change." From here we will move to a discussion of the materials and methods used in our work with *The Mothers of Change.*

What is a Mother Goddess?

I call this sacromagical series *The Mothers of Change*, as opposed to *The Goddesses of Change* because it is my intention to invite the maternal attributes of the spiritual "Mothers" of us all. In the context of the Divine Feminine quartet known as Maiden, Mother, Queen and Crone, four uniquely different aspects or faces of the feminine are highlighted and revered. Here, Mother represents the maternal, care-giving aspect of her eternal presence.

To be clear, in this work no distinction is made between a spiritual Mother and an otherworldly Goddess; they are one and the same. Five of the six *Mothers of Change* have always been venerated by their patron cultures as Mothers and Goddesses. Miryam, though once human, has through her nature and deeds, been elevated to the status of a Goddess. Please note, for ease I will combine the terms Mother and Goddess into a unified "Mother Goddess" henceforth; again emphasizing the fact that in this work no distinction is made between the two.

"Goddess" and "Mother" are terms that many use, but few define. In our modern spiritual revival the term is more often defined by its use and associations than its literal or practical nature. Thus we must begin our work here, by clarifying exactly who or what is a Mother or Goddess?

A Goddess or Mother is a culture's way of identifying, relating to and honoring the primal powers of creation, through a part human-part Divine feminine form.

Because this definition sets the stage for all that follows, let's take the time to examine each aspect included herein.

The physical form of a Mother Goddess is benevolently built by her culture as a means of personifying, and thus better relating to, the abstract spiritual powers of the Cosmos. In this, she is shaped to become a fitting vessel for the particular powers she mediates to and for her people. This "shaping" includes all aspects of her physical and metaphysical nature; such as her clothing, adornments, tools, posture and the manner in which her altars and temples are constructed. Enhanced by an accumulation of prayers, thought forms, incantations and material offerings, the metaphysical form of a Mother Goddess becomes a spiritual storehouse of reverence and power. Further, the power within her image, stored in the astral plane, is readily available to indwell wherever her physical form (i.e. statue, temple or shrine) resides and appropriate enriching observances take place.

This leads us to an important understanding of how a Mother Goddess functions spiritually. Consider again her image, built by those who revere and seek to better understand the primal powers of creation she mediates. *Behind* her image we find the primal powers themselves: impersonal forces of the Cosmos informing all life and flowing through her into the world of form. *Before* her image we find the reverent acts of humanity: statues, rituals, temples and offerings as well as the human emotions, prayers and incantations that focus and magnify the power she mediates. *Within* her image the two conjoin, as the primal powers of creation and the human reverence of those powers come together as one.

All Mother Goddesses personify and mediate particular spiritual powers of the unseen worlds that are, nearly always, a function of the Four-Fold Nature of Creation: namely the elements of Air, Fire, Water and Earth. Though they may contain traces of a tempering or secondary element (e.g. a warm fire versus a raging blaze or a rain shower versus a hurricane), most Mother Goddesses are uni-elemental. As part human-part Divine beings, Mother Goddesses mediate the spiritual power of the element to which they are aligned. In this, they help us to receive and work with the physical and spiritual qualities of that element. For example, those who inspire, instruct and mentor human evolution such as Athena and Isis, mediate the elemental power of Air and East; for the Divine impulses that inspire our minds, communication, poetry and song dwell in the East/Air[1]. Likewise, the fires of purification and initiation are aligned with the spiritual powers of the South/Fire. The Mother Goddesses who mediate these powers, such as Sekhmet and Pele, are thusly attributed.

Over time, humanity will undoubtedly progress to the point where we are able to work directly with the primal powers behind the Mother Goddesses without their mediating forms. For now, we should be grateful for the spiritual reservoirs our ancestors of blood and spirit created for us in inspiring and vivifying these Mother Goddess forms.

The temples of ancient civilizations are often misunderstood by our modern mind, thus I would also like to take a moment to clarify their purpose as you will visit three temples associated with *The Mothers of Change*.

The temples of ancient civilizations were storehouses of food, valuables and other commodities in common ownership. The Goddess or God in residence was the protector of the community's livelihood. It was believed that the offerings and rituals done in their honor sustained this protection. It is often reported in archeological research that temples were seldom robbed or looted in the ancient world for fear of retribution from the patron God or Goddess. Exceptions to this occurred under circumstances of invasion by foreign entities seeking to conquer and/or enslave the community. What better way to destroy a community's cohesiveness than by desecrating its sacred shrines and temples? Though we consider ourselves to be more advanced than our human ancestors, the tribal practice of "hitting a community where it lives spiritually" is still used today.

To be clear, all that has been said here with regard to the nature of the Mother Goddesses applies to the Father Gods as well. As the Father Gods possess the seeds of creation, as opposed to the womb of creation, their role in our spiritual and material lives is different. Taking into account their unique spiritual attributes, a model of working with *The Fathers of Change* could also be created. Though I've worked with the Divine Feminine for many years, it has always been done under the aegis of the Sacred Marriage, which I feel must be our common plea. When we learn to truly honor and merge the feminine and masculine creative forces with the Four-Fold Nature of Creation, we have a complete map of the ordering of the Cosmos alive within us. In preparation, let us learn the way of *The Mothers* and in so doing welcome the coming forth of the benevolent *Fathers* and their ultimate Sacred Union.

What is Change?

All life, all forces and all forms are composed of four "roots" or "elements;" they are Air, Fire, Water and Earth. When considering the unmanifest, we may include a fifth element, aether, as well. This which Empedocles proclaimed in his metaphysical poem entitled, *On Nature* circa 470 BCE has become the basis for many spiritual and magical systems. Though credited with the first written record of the four roots, it is likely that the great Greek metaphysician inherited this sacromagical taxonomy from his own teachers, and they from theirs. Nevertheless, it was Empedocles that put forth the notion that the formation, structure, and history of the Universe as a whole (both material and intangible) was steered by an omnipresent co-creation of Air, Fire, Water and Earth (again, the Four-Fold Nature of Creation.)

Empedocles explained all four roots are found in all things in various combinations and proportions. Yet we can be certain that each retains its own unique essence and force, even when combined with the others. He also told us that these four roots are motivated or moved by two opposing Cosmic forces: Love and Strife. Love creates attraction and Strife repulsion or separation among the roots; together variation and harmony emerge. Empedocles associated and identified the four primary roots of creation with particular patron Gods/Goddesses. In his system, Zeus mediates the power of Air, while Hera empowers Earth. Nestis (referring also to Persephone/Proserpina) infuses the Waters and Aidoneus (i.e. Hades) the Fires.

What Empedocles initiated with regard to the Four-Fold Nature of Creation was inherited and expanded upon by Socrates, Plato, Aristotle and Plotinus. In fact, it was Plato who first coined the phrase "four elements," used today in place of Empedocles' "four roots." With this understanding as to how the magical four elements of the created world were first acknowledged within written records preserved to date, let us again address our initial question: "What is change?"

It was said previously that all four roots are found in all things in various combinations and proportions; however, each retains its own unique properties and purposes. When the combination or relationship between the elements remains relatively constant, the manifest forms composed by Air, Fire, Water and Earth remain constant as well. However, when the proportional relationship among them changes (i.e. the prominence of Water gives way to Fire, Earth or Air), the manifest form they co-create changes as well.

Change is created by the reordering of the elements.

As the proportion of Earth to Water and Air to Fire fluctuates, old patterns and influences are released and new patterns and influences come into form. What's more, these changes occur first in the Divine templates of the unseen worlds before they become manifest in the physical world of form.

Because the temporal Mother Goddesses mediate the power of the elements, in real time (from moment to moment, never ceasing), through their part human-part Divine feminine form, they also mediate the changes of the elements as they occur. Thus, when we work with these Mother Goddesses and the powers they mediate, we receive intimations and whispers of the changes to come. Simply put, our meditations with *The Mothers of Change* enable us to recognize, receive and work with change as it materializes!

If we wait for the physical manifestations of change, we see and receive the last leg of their progression or evolution. If instead we attune to the unseen realms where the intimations of change begin, we may see and sense the initial and continual impulses of change and can thus better prepare for and co-create with the manifest form as it materializes.

It must be said that *The Mothers of Change* give of themselves and that which they meditate to sincere and unfettered hearts, according to our true needs. If we seek to attune to the forces of change for our own exclusive benefit, we can be sure that much will be withheld from us. To do this work to its and our utmost, we must create and maintain within ourselves a be-nevolent, service-oriented way of thinking, feeling and being. Only then will the higher and deeper knowledge be entrusted to us.

Practical Work with The Mothers of Change

The methods applied to our work with *The Mothers of Change* are primarily meditative. In this, two techniques are employed; one is stillness and the other attunement. When used together these two techniques work to strengthen our greatest sacromagical tool which is not any physical object we lay upon our altars, but instead, our own consciousness.

Stillness is the meditation form used to release all prior occupations and come into a place of mental, physical and emotional quiet and receptivity. Its aim is to render us physically tranquil, emotionally calm and spiritually receptive. Unless we are capable of lessening the frequency and turning down the volume of our own thoughts, perceptions and feelings, we cannot hope to hear, see and feel the subtle realms. Stillness meditation is also referred to as passive meditation; again for the receptive state in which it places us. There are many different means to achieve stillness; they are as varied as the spiritual practices that espouse them. In your work with *The Mothers of Change*, you are welcome to use any method that fosters a quiet and receptive state of being. If you are new to the concept of a stillness practice, there are two stillness meditations offered for you to explore toward the end of the book.

The second meditative method we will draw upon is attunement. Attunement is a meditation technique of purposeful orientation and direction. In attunement meditation we focus our awareness upon a particular principle, being or energy, creating a circuit of force between our own consciousness and the consciousness of the principle, being or energy.

To understand this meditative concept, compare yourself to an electrical appliance. The electrical socket into which you plug yourself enables electricity to flow through a cord and into you. Through this physical "connection" you are energized. Attunement meditations function in much the same way. As men and women of spirit, we may be spiritually and physically energized (i.e. purified, healed, transformed, inspired, uplifted and the like) by "plugging ourselves into" particularly chosen spiritual reservoirs. We do this by focusing our consciousness upon those reservoirs. In the current context, the chosen spiritual reservoirs into which we will plug (or attune) ourselves are *The Mothers of Change.* In doing so, we will be energized, healed, transformed, inspired and uplifted via the primal forces of creation that they mediate.

With consistent practice over time, attunement meditations foster deep states of communion through which human and Divine beings may forge life-long partnerships. Due to the focus and work involved, attunement is also referred to as active meditation.

The attunement meditations used in *The Mothers of Change* were created in communion with each Mother Goddess. Based upon my own research into their cultural iconography and mythos, these workings fuse together the creative forces each Mother Goddess mediates with the time-tested meditation techniques used within the Western Esoteric systems of the Northern Hemisphere.

Declaring Our Sacred Need

We always begin our work with *The Mothers of Change* by determining and defining *our sacred need*. In other words, for what specific and important purpose do we choose to consult them now? By what aspects of personal and/or transpersonal change are we being currently challenged? As you work to determine what it is that you need from the Mothers now, take care to delve deeply, moving past the surface concerns and into the pith and marrow at the center of your current struggle. In other words, let your sacred need unfold through true inner inquiry.

Once we've clearly defined (and recorded on paper) our sacred need, we are ready to proceed. Along these lines we must remember this: what we understand as our sacred need may be superseded by the vast intelligence and omnipresent awareness of *The Mothers* themselves. So although we may formulate a clear understanding of our own need based upon our perceptions of change, the ultimate authority as to *our true sacred need* is theirs and theirs alone.

With our sacred need defined to the best of our ability, we are ready to move into the meditations that enable our contact and communion with each of the six *Mothers of Change*. We may do this in one long or several shorter sessions, whichever way is most fitting to our life circumstances at the time.

The Mothers' Chant and Meditations

Like the elemental forces they mediate, *The Mothers of Change* work in harmony as a collective; thus forming a unified three-dimensional sphere of Divine influence and guidance. The diagram below illustrates this sphere in two-dimensional form, as seen from above.

Using our imagination, we may envision this form in three-dimensions by dividing the center circle into two circles so that Anankê is a point above and Orchil a point below the other four *Mothers*. The human being occupying the center is surrounded front, back, left and right by the four temporal Mother Goddesses, each in their respective directions, with Orchil founding and Anankê crowning the spherical form. I refer to this three-dimensional form as the *Holy Sphere of Unification*. Though we focus our attentions and attunements on each Mother Goddess in our exploratory meditations, in truth they exist in co-creation at all times (just like the elements whose power they mediate.) A sensory appreciation of the inherent beauty and harmony of their Divine co-creation is resonant within *The Mothers' Chant*, which I will now describe.

Near the beginning of *The Mothers of Change* CD, there is a sung chant consisting of the consonants and vowels that begin the name of each Mother Goddess. These sounds are arranged in the same order as their meditative progression, moving Sun-wise from the Underworld to the Overworld, and concluding with a unifying "ohm" as follows.

Mother Goddess	Position	Sound
Orchil	Underworld	O as "oh"
Athena	East	A as "ā"
Sekhmet	South	Se as "say"
Miryam	West	Mi as "me"
Inanna	North	I as "ee"
Anankê	Overworld	An as "on"
Unification	Holy Sphere	Ohm

This chant was created for use at the commencement of each and every *Mothers of Change* meditation; however on the companion CD is it recorded only once, at the beginning of the disk. This was done to ensure that your own, individual chanting begins each sacromagical working (versus a recorded chant.) Thus please sing the chant on your own, prior to each *Mothers of Change* incantation and subsequent meditation.

The chant holds present the unique place each *Mother of Change* possesses, as well as the unity of their collective impact within the *Holy Sphere of Unification*. Like any sacred chant, though you will hear and feel its power the first time you sing it, with time and repeated use, it will become a stronger and stronger means of sensing and receiving *The Mothers,* both individually and collectively.

In addition to our work with *The Mothers'* meditations, the chant can be used anytime you wish to be reunited with the spiritual presence of *The Mothers of Change*. The chant will be helpful when, in some particularly challenging moment, you need to recall prior guidance given. It may also be used as a means of keeping your daily consciousness attuned to and aware of the constancy of their Divine presence.

The Organization of this Book

The book is organized in such as way as to provide consistent and comparable information among *The Mothers*. Each section begins with the cultural origination of the Mother Goddess herself, followed by comparable attributes such as her pantheon, historical context, symbols, religious/spiritual observances, esoteric attributes and the like. Please note, the information contained in this section is only intended to provide a basic and reliable cultural and historical reference. On its own, this information will not impart an enduring knowledge and understanding of the Mother Goddesses themselves; it is instead a means of aligning your consciousness at the starting point. The real work of "knowing and understanding," is not achieved through intellectual fact-gathering. To know them, we must go out to meet them through active meditation. To know them we must forge a communal relationship; there are no shortcuts... there are no other ways.

After reading the section that relays their historical and cultural attributes, you will see the magical incantation written for each *Mother of Change*. Though included as a means of opening the way prior your meditative workings, the incantations may be used in other settings as well, for instance in prayer or ritual outside your formal work with *The Mothers of Change* meditations. Five of the six incantations are my own; the incantation to Orchil was written by Fiona Macleod.

After the incantation, you will come at last to the text of the meditation that guides your work with the Mother Goddesses. Each of these forms was created, in the age-old fashion wherein we, as human Priestesses or Priests, are inspired to pave the way for others to follow, according to the directives of our otherworldly guides. Thus each of these six meditations was created in close relationship with the powers behind them, namely

The Mothers themselves. Once you've learned to find your way to them, using either the printed or recorded versions of these meditations, your sacred imagination and body memory will retain this visceral knowledge. Thus you may only need the CD initially, until you have memorized the forms.

The Sacromagical Form

You may perform *The Mothers of Change* meditations in single, consecutive or long, continuous sessions. The instructions that follow assume a long, continuous pattern. If you are working in shorter, individual sessions, you will start each working by aligning your candle and sacred need with *The Mother of Change* to whom you now journey.

First, purchase or make a dedicated candle for use in your work with *The Mothers of Change*. It is best for your candle to be unscented, as some meditative experiences with *The Mothers* may involve the reception of subtle smells; a scented candle will negate this transference.

To begin your work, determine your relationship to the four directions of East, South, West and North. Beginning with Orchil in the Underworld, place your new, unscented candle in the direction associated with this Mother Goddess: central and under. As your mediations progress, you will move your candle to the East for Athena, South for Sekhmet, West for Miryam and North for Inanna. The placement for Anankê should be central and over. Once your candle is placed in the direction of the Mother Goddess to whom you will now journey, lay your sacred need (written on a small piece of paper) at the base of your candle. As you do this, envision yourself placing this paper at the feet of the *Mother of Change* you are now to meet.

With this preparation complete, enter a minute or two of stillness to simultaneously clear, purify and ready yourself to receive this Mother Goddess. Please note, on the CD that accompanies this book, the stillness prompt and following quiet time is brief. Please use the "pause" button on your CD player to determine the period of stillness you require.

After the stillness prompt, sing *The Mothers of Change* chant. Following this speak, or if using the CD release "pause" to receive, the incantation to the *Mother of Change*. From here, the guided meditation will lead you into and out from your communion with the particular Mother Goddess. Once you've returned to the world of form, journal your impressions and any instruction she offered to you. To continue, move your candle and sacred need clockwise and begin again. To aid you in the sequence here again are the steps:

- Orient to the appropriate direction/element,
- Place and light your candle,
- Place your sacred need (written) before the candle,
- Enter stillness,
- Sing The Mothers' Chant,
- Speak/play the Incantation,
- Follow the Visionary Meditation.

The meditations (as recorded) vary from eleven to fifteen minutes in length. With appropriate time built in for your own pauses and still points, you should be able to complete each meditation within twenty to twenty-five minutes. Again, please use the "pause" button on your CD player to determine your individual silence or quiet time requirements.

Through each of the six attunement meditations, we travel partway toward each *Mother of Change* in their dwelling place within the unseen worlds, as is our duty. They, in turn, come part way to us; and thus a real and enduring communion may evolve. It is through this communion that clear guidance and direction comes to us according to our true needs. In addition to guidance and direction, we may also receive tiny, homeopathic infusions of the power they mediate. These infusions are received directly into our subtle and physical bodies. Over time, they gently transform us from the inside; and thus often occur beyond, and in spite of, our mental understanding and conditioning.

Though not mandatory, I have found it helpful to make a physical offering to each Mother as I begin my work with her. Normally this consists of a specially chosen cup of wine, beer, tea, cake or other small hand-made food item. At the conclusion of the working, I place this offering within the Earth where it will continue to nourish the planet she cares for through her Divine presence.

When you've completed your work with all six Mothers, whether in one continuous session or over several days' sessions, take the time to review each of the journal entries from all six meditations. Let the continuity of the co-parentage of these six Mother Goddesses emerge and take form, allowing you to see and sense what you need to do to integrate, employ and embody their guidance.

Though all hold a piece of the puzzle for us every time we journey to meet them, you may find that one Mother Goddess offers specific keys for you in the face of the particular sacred need you now carry. Thus you may decide to continue working with her in a direct manner, perhaps creating an altar for her, to better enable and focus your further work. If you remember that change is the reordering of the elements, it stands to reason that as we change, there may be a leading direction/element driving our own "reordering," thus there may also be one Mother Goddess whose change imperative guides your way forward.

A Sincere Invitation

With all that has proceeded as our introduction and foundation, it is with great sincerity that I invite you to begin your work with *The Mothers of Change.* May the depth, insight, precision, compassion, vitality and perspective of these six great Mothers bless you in preparation for your journey forward in life. May their constancy, surrounding and permeating all we are and will become, forever guide you in times of change, great and small.

Orchil

Orchil

Cultural Origins: Created by Fiona Macleod,
18th Century Scottish faery/trans-human mystic and poet,
through William Sharp her human partner.

Sources: *The Silence of Amor Where the Forest Whispers*, 1895
Ula and Urla from *Washer of the Ford*, 1896-1899 and
The Awakening of Angus Òg from *The Winged Destiny: Studies in
the Spiritual History of the Gael*, 1911.

Goddess of: the Underworld who sits in a vast cavern weaving
at the looms of life and death. With one hand she weaves life
upward into the surface world and toward the Stars; with the
other hand she weaves death downward through layers of the
decomposing soils, toward the center of the Earth. Orchil is the
Weaver Goddess of corporeal form. "The one whom the Druids
knew."

Pantheon & Cultural Mythos: Orchil does not belong to a cultural pantheon. She originates from the Scottish Highland poetic cycle initiated by Fiona Macleod in the late 1800s within
Scottish and Irish Gaelic tradition.

In nature, orchil is a lichen-derived substance that, once fer-
mented, becomes a purple die used to color wool. It is also the
name of a castle in Perthshire, Scotland.

Fiona Macleod was a faery/trans-human Scottish mystic, ex-
pressed exclusively through her relationship to the Scottish author, William Sharp (1855 – 1905.) As an inner feminine being
of the otherworlds, Fiona was at one with the mind and heart of
faery. Her exquisite and haunting poetry, stories and dramas
left an indelible mark upon Scottish folklore and Celtic spiritu-
ality. The following quotation taken from R.J. Stewart's essay

William Sharp and the Esoteric Orders further elucidates this magical part human-part Divine co-creation.

> *"William Sharp was inspired by an inner feminine conscious-*
> *ness, Fiona Macleod. He described her sometimes as an ances-*
> *tral seeress. Today we would call her, perhaps, an inner con-*
> *tact, and at a deeper level, the Goddess within. In this sense he*
> *embodied in person many of the deep changes of sexuality to-*
> *wards androgyny that are occurring today. It was not an easy*
> *embodiment for him, in the repressed 19th century. For a time*
> *the book-buying public thought that William Sharp and Fiona*
> *Macleod were separate persons. When he came out and admit-*
> *ted to being both, there was a scandal."*
>
> - R.J. Stewart, 2007

The poetic incantation to *Orchil* was published in 1895 in Fiona Macleod's *The Silence of Amor Where the Forest Whispers* in the following manner:

> *"I dreamed of Orchil, the dim goddess who is under the brown*
> *earth, in a vast cavern, where she weaves at two looms. With*
> *one hand she weaves life upward through the grass; with the*
> *other she weaves death downward through the mould; and the*
> *sound of the weaving is Eternity, and the name of it in the*
> *green world is Time. And, through all, Orchil weaves the weft*
> *of Eternal Beauty, that passeth not, though its soul is Change.*
> *This is my comfort, O Beauty that art of Time, who am faint*
> *and hopeless in the strong sound of that other weaving, where*
> *Orchil, the dim goddess, sits dreaming at her loom under the*
> *brown earth."*

What was originally written as a powerful incantation for the Weaver Goddess of the Underworld, was later set in prose in *Ula and Urla* published in *The Washer of the Ford* (Patrick Geddes 1896, re-issued again by David Nutt 1899) In this riveting story of unrequited love, Isla recalls the words of Maol the Druid who told him of Orchil, the dim Goddess who lives under the brown Earth. The words he uses are the same as those offered in the prior poetic incantation.

In *The Awakening of Angus Òg* from *The Winged Destiny: Studies in the Spiritual History of the Gael* (published in 1895, an edition published in 1913 by William Heineman is available at Sundown Shores) we find this haunting reference to Orchil which begins the saga of the long sleep of Angus Òg imposed by Orchil who gives and takes his awakeness in the green world.

> *"Yet there were eyes to see, for Orchil lifted her gaze from where she dreamed her triune dream beneath the heather. The goddess ceased from her weaving at the looms of life and death, and looked broodingly at Angus Òg--Angus, the fair god, the ever-young, the lord of love, of music, of song.*
>
> *Is it time that he slept indeed?" she murmured, after a long while, wherein she felt the sudden blood redden her lips and the pulse in her quiet veins leap like a caged bird. But while she still pondered this thing, three old Druids came over the shoulder of the hill, and advanced slowly to where the Yellow-haired One lay adream. These, however, she knew to be no mortals, but three of the ancient gods.*
>
> *When they came upon Angus Òg they sought to wake him, but Orchil had breathed a breath across a granite rock and blown the deep immemorial age of it upon him, so that even the speech of the elder gods was no more in his ears than a gnat's idle rumour."*

As both poem and prose indicate, Orchil, the Weaver Goddess of the Underworld composes and decomposes physical form. As such, her skill and authority are ever-present and unquestionable, encompassing all within the green world. As we have read, her might is even greater than the old Gods whose Druids endeavored in vain to wake beloved Angus Òg, the ever-young God of love and death.

The writings extolling the power and evoking the presence of Orchil are but samples of the many wonderful stories, dramas and poems from the life and mystical works of William Sharp and Fiona Macleod. To better understand this Mother Goddess, in the context of her magical and all-enthralling creation, here are three recommended sources for your further exploration:

- Steve Blamires extensively researched and well-written biography of William Sharp: *The Little Book of the Great Enchantment, R.J. Stewart Books, 2008.*

- R.J. Stewart's intensive workshop *The Faery Magic of Fiona Macleod* and writings such as *William Sharp and the Esoteric Orders* are available at {www.dreampower.com/ fiona_macleod. com.}

- Mary Ann Dobratz's website *Sundown Shores* located at {www.sundown.pair.com} chronicling much the life's works of William Sharp and Fiona Macleod.

Religious/Spiritual Observations: Orchil is a Weaver Goddess of the Underworld; it is she who bequeaths to us the flesh and bones of the physical body upon our birth. At our death, these same physical components of our corporeal nature are returned unto her. The religious/spiritual observances of the Weaver Goddesses occur within many indigenous and pagan traditions. Weaver Goddesses, such as Spider Woman, Frigg and Arachne spin the threads of life and creativity. In addition to weaving the tapestry of physical life, Weaver Goddesses also possess the gift of prophecy. Orchil is unique among the Weaver Goddesses for her looms reside in the Underworld, where the physical components of life and death originate.

Symbols & Esoteric Attributes: two looms, weaving, caves or caverns, life and death, the Underworld.

Orchil is a *Mother of Change* because she presides over the cycles of life and death throughout all eternity. Granting us the physical form at the commencement of each life, and taking back this form at our death. In this she weaves the ultimate change of embodiment and disembodiment at her two looms.

Invocation to Orchil

By Fiona Macleod

I dreamed of Orchil,
The dim Goddess,
Who is under the brown Earth,
In a vast cavern,
Where she weaves at two looms.
With one hand she weaves life
Upward through the grass;
With the other she weaves death,
downward through the mould.

And the sound of the weaving is Eternity,
And the name of it in the green world is Time.

And, through all,
Orchil weaves the weft of Eternal Beauty,
That passeth not,
Though its soul is Change.

This is my comfort,
O Beauty that art of Time,
Who am faint and hopeless,
In the strong sound of that other weaving,
Where Orchil,
The dim Goddess,
Sits dreaming at her loom,
Under the brown Earth.

Meditation for Orchil

Begin by coming into stillness and releasing all prior occupations of mind and body.

To find her...we must let go of our attachment to life.
To find her...we must let go of our attachment to death.
For through all...Orchil weaves the weft of eternal Beauty... eternal Beauty that passeth not...though its soul is Change.

See yourself...see your life...wrapped in the beautiful weaving of Orchil's looms; rich in earthen colors of sienna, gold, russet and deep green. See each thread she's woven to uphold and support you.

Search among the threads that bind you to this physical form. Search until you find the single gossamer, black thread that stands alone among the threads of color.

When you die, this is the thread she pulls...to unravel your body...and release your spirit. With the same ease with which we might unravel a scarf by pulling one thread; Orchil pulls the black thread within us, gathering all other colors back unto her.

This opalescent black thread, rich as the iridescent crow's feathers, connects you always to her. Touch this thread found woven within the strands of your life's weaving.

Soon you will pull this thread of your own strength....not *from your center* as she will one day pull, but *toward* your center...in life...not death. It is this motion that allows us to return to her while fully alive.

Remember *your sacred need* ... call it clearly to your mind.

Then…pull upon the black thread of Orchil's looms…pull and gather the slack…as you do, see the Earth slip open beneath you…wet and heavy…dark and smooth.

Feel the cool, thick, mud envelop you as you continue to pull upon the black thread of Orchil's looms.

Eyes covered in blackness…ears thick with the sounds of the deep cavernous Earth…pull upon the thread of Orchil's looms.

Breath from nowhere…feet unfeeling ground…pull upon the thread of Orchil's looms. Senses lost within an impenetrable, rich darkness….pull upon the thread of Orchil's looms.

Darkness…opening…dimness of light returning…holding her thread in your mud-encrusted hands see before you the first loom of Orchil with a multitude of threads reaching upward into the brown Earth each thread a life, woven by her skillful hands.

See before you the second loom of Orchil with a multitude of threads reaching downward from the brown Earth, each thread a death, woven by her skillful hands.

Clear your eyes of their molded sight. See the fast movement of her bone-white hands, skillfully passing the shuttle back and forth through the looms. Listen to the sounds of Eternity woven upon Orchil's two looms…listen to the sound of your own life's weaving, among the multitude of threads.

You will never see her face while you live…but you may hear her voice echoing through the vast cavern of your own heart as she speaks to you now according to *your sacred need* of this and the coming times.

Commune with Orchil, the dim Goddess of the Underworld, in silence.

Silence

With this…your time here ends…look about you…searching now for the thread of your favorite color; this is the thread of your most precious nature. Let the coils of the black thread that guided you here stay piled at your feet while you pull upon the thread of your most precious nature.

Darkness returning….Earth enveloping…pull upon the thread of your most precious nature. Thickness of breath…blindness of eye…pull upon the thread of your most precious nature.

Richness of fertile creativity and deep soils life force…pull upon the thread of your most precious nature.

Pull upon this thread….until the rich, dark Earth spits you out of its mouth and back among the many colors of Orchil's life weaving.

See again, the black thread of death…tucked neatly into the form of your life, among the many colors of you.

With each breath in….and each breath out…fan the bellows of your lungs…let these rising winds within bring alive your waking consciousness, in full possession of all she's given you…Here…Now.

Athena

Athena

Cultural Origins: Ancient Libya (as Neith)
Etruscan/Ancient Italy (as Minerva), Crete in 4000 BCE,
Known to Ancient Greeks through the works of
Hesiod and Homer circa 700 BCE.

Goddess of: war, civilization, wisdom, strength, strategy, crafts, justice, skill, hunting, weaving, philosophy and metal working. Inventor of the plow, rake, bridle, chariot, ox yoke, flute and trumpet.

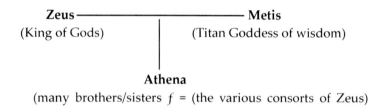

Zeus		**Metis**
(King of Gods)		(Titan Goddess of wisdom)

Athena
(many brothers/sisters f = (the various consorts of Zeus)

Pantheon & Cultural Mythos: Athena's cult dates from the earliest of times. In Mycenaean mythology she appears before her father Zeus, while in Olympian mythology, she is his favorite daughter. In other myths she is Zeus' sister, which indicates she is older than, or at least as old as, he. Her origins as a pre-Greek Goddess explain the mythological depictions of her birth, emerging fully formed from the head of her father.

Plato identified her with the Libyan Warrior Goddess Neith of Sais in Ancient Egypt. Athena's horse haired helmet is reminiscent of the appearance of the pre-Greek Neith, and still older Minerva of the Etruscan culture (pre-Roman civilization dating from 800-300 BCE in what is now Tuscany.)

Athena is often given the epithet "Tritogeneia" meaning either "of Titan born" or "third born" as referenced in the *Iliad*, the *Homeric Hymns* and Hesiod's *Theogony*. In fact, there are several versions of her birth story, the most famous being the union of Zeus with the Titan Goddess Metis.

The story begins with Zeus being warned that his progeny would seize his authority and thus become more powerful than he. To avoid this fate, he ate his first wife, the Titan Goddess Metis. However Metis was already pregnant. As the baby's birth neared, Zeus began complaining of headaches and called for Hephaestus, his son the blacksmith, to split open his head for relief. With this, Athena burst forth fully armed with the weapons given to her by her mother, Metis.

Athena is often referred to as "Pallas Athena." In one account of the origin of this name, Pallas was a childhood friend of Athena's. One day when the two were playing, unwitting of her own strength, Athena accidentally killed Pallas. To honor her fallen friend, she set Pallas' name before her own. In a different account, Pallas was said to be Athena's father, a winged goat-like giant. When he attempted to outrage her, she stripped him of his goat-skinned aegis[2] and took his name.

In the Olympian mythological cycle, with the fickle and prolific Zeus as her father, Athena had many brothers and sisters. Of special interest to us, are her brothers Ares/Mars and Hephaestus/Vulcan; for through these two relationships we come to understand her nature as a Goddess of war and virginity, respectively.

Many do not understand the unique disposition Athena possesses as a Goddess of war, intellect and cunning. This aspect of her nature is best understood when compared to that of her brother Ares. Ares is described in the Greek hymns as being magnanimous, unconquered and boisterous. He is the raw, un tamable force of bloody war. In contrast, Athena is the cunning, intellect and wisdom applied to inevitable conflict. In all stories, she is said to dislike fighting and refuses to do so without a purpose. Where Ares is readily provoked, Athena prefers to settle disputes without bloodshed through the application of wisdom and logic.

As a virgin Goddess, Athena retains her virtue and thus becomes neither lover nor mother. Again, the manner in which she retains her chastity is best understood through story.

Athena's brother Hephaestus is manipulated by her arch-rival Poseidon in an attempt to usurp her maidenhood and thus disgrace her. As was referenced before, Hephaestus is the God of blacksmiths and metallurgy. One day, Athena asked him to fashion a set of arms for her. Prior to the completion of the armor, Poseidon told Hephaestus that Athena was on her way to see him and was, with Zeus' consent, hoping for violent passion. Prompted by Poseidon's lascivious lies, Hephaestus refuses payment for his work, saying he wanted only to love her in return for this labors. Normally well-behaved, he thrust himself upon her. As she pushed him away, he ejaculated on her leg. This she quickly wiped off with sheep's wool and threw to the ground. From the seed of Hephaestus and the fertile Earth, a child was formed named Erichthonius. Not wanting Poseidon to have the satisfaction of a successful scheme, Athena hid the child in a basket and gave him to a foster mother thus again demonstrating her compassionate reason.

Her mercy is great and always applied in situations where other Goddesses have exacted a much greater punishment. For instance, when Teiresias accidentally catches her in a bath (and thus sees her naked which is expressly forbidden,) she blinds him; and at the behest of his Mother, gives him the gift of inward sight as compensation. Thus Teiresias becomes a great seer and prophet.

There are many stories highlighting Athena's love of humanity and her dedication to its social evolution. She helps Odysseus in Homer's *Odyssey* as the inner voice that guides him during his grave and treacherous journey. She helps Jason by instructing him to build a ship called the Argo with a magical prophetic wood that advises the crew in securing the Golden Fleece and thus the throne of Pelias. She helps Heracles during several of his twelve labors, which he must undergo in atonement for the killing of his family. Finally, she helps Prometheus by enabling him to bring fire to humanity. As this story bears special significance for our work, let us expand upon this example of Athena's helpful nature.

Athena was endeared with the race of man and thus wished to help in all its true and righteous endeavors. Zeus, on the other hand, was not enamored with the human race. As king of the Gods, he forbade all other Gods from sharing knowledge with humans which, via the acquisition of particular skills and abilities, would serve their advancement. In opposition to her father's wishes, Athena devised a plan whereby humanity would receive holy wisdom without violating the laws of Zeus. She summoned Prometheus, one of the Titans, (pre-Olympian deities) to whom she taught the ways of wisdom. As Prometheus was not an Olympian God (but instead a Titan), Athena was not prevented from teaching him and Prometheus was not prevented by Zeus from sharing his knowledge with humans.

Athena advised Prometheus by showing him the secret entrance to the chamber on Mt. Olympus which housed the Chariot of the Sun at night. Prometheus took a pithy fennel stalk and under the cover of darkness, lit his make-shift torch from the flaming Chariot. He then extinguished the flame, leaving only a glowing ember ensuring the captive fire would not be seen as he left the hall. When Prometheus returned to Earth, he blew upon the ember to rekindle the torch, giving fire and all it offers, to humanity.

One final important story, from Plato's *Menexenus*, describes the manner in which Athens received its name. As a nameless city-state, its primary benefactors were Athena and Poseidon. Thus it was decided that both would present their people with a gift; the gift the people accepted indicated who would become the city-state's namesake.

In a demonstration of his gift to the people, Poseidon struck the ground with his trident producing a valuable spring that would grant them trade (as an eventual river,) consumable water and fish. Athena presented the people with an olive tree, thus offering wood, oil and food to all. On close examination, we can see that Poseidon's gift, being trade-related, continued the people's reliance on others. Athena's gift offered the means of independent prosperity. Seeing the distinct advantage of her offering, the people chose Athena's gift and namesake.

For Plato this was an especially strategic story, for it was time for the people to move away from the older stories of ever-warring Gods and Goddesses. Both Socrates and Plato witnessed the historic myths being interpreted in too literal a manner, and thus condoning humanity's bad acts. After all, these acts of righteous vengeance were nothing less than that which the Gods committed themselves. Both Socrates and Plato endeavored to relay the deeper meaning behind the myths thus lifting their coarse, literal interpretation. In this, Plato was careful to narrate the naming of Athens through a non-combative means. Moreover, he skillfully replaced the old Atlantean magical hierarchy with Athena's wisdom, justice and shared prosperity.

Finally, Plato, Herodotus and Diodorus Siculus identified Athena with the Goddess Neith who was the patron deity of the Ancient Egyptian city of Sais. In this, an important link was fused between Athens and Sais; as Sais was said to survive the deluge that toppled Atlantis. Thus through the early philosophers' witty expositions, the stage was set for the ideals of Athena to be foundational in Greece; and for her namesake, to be in full possession of that which was preserved when Atlantis fell (i.e. Sais and the lineage of its patron Goddess.)

Religious/Spiritual Observations: Athena's temple was the Parthenon built on the Acropolis in Athens, 448-438 BCE. Designed on a flat-topped rock, the Parthenon rose one hundred and fifty feet above the sea, exuding the qualities of symmetry and the balance of individual freedom with common aims.

Though now in ruins, we can still see the rectangular building's skeletal symmetry, open on all sides in an invitation to those who would revere the Goddess within. The yet visible pedimental imagery above the West entrance depicts the contest between Athena and Poseidon; while the imagery above the East entrance illustrates her birth.

The naos or cella inside the temple housed a forty-two foot statue of Athena holding the Goddess Nike (the likeness of which may not be seen in the Parthenon replica in Nashville, Tennessee.) The smaller room located behind the naos, called the opisthodomos, was used as a treasury. The frieze running along the upper edge of the temple wall depicted a procession of horsemen, musicians, animals and other ritualized figures.

Symbols and Esoteric Attributes: owl, aegis with gorgon's head and tassels of pure gold, battle shield, snake, bird wings, helmet adorned with horse hair. Grey-eyed Goddess, bright-eyed, protectress of heroes. Goddess of nearness, thinking and intellect. Goddess of the East and the powers of Instruction and Inspiration within the body of Archangel Raphael.

Athena is a *Mother of Change* because she valiantly and virtuously aids humanity in its quest for advancement, enabling our heroes and heroines to move beyond the thresholds of uncertainty and inability for the greater good of the communities they serve. In addition, she employs both might and mercy, two important qualities to hold in the balance during times of great change.

Incantation to Athena

Athena, grey-eyed Goddess of unbending heart,
Whose birth would not be quelled,
By a jealous father's art.

Spring forth,
As you once did from Zeus' crown,
In service to those who would,
make themselves a life renowned.

Goddess of nearness,
As with Odysseus,
Fill our minds with cunning, pure;
Protectress,
As with Prometheus,
Shield our fire's ardor.

Tritogeneia, of Titan lineage bright,
Teach us when to gain by mercy,
And when to gain by might.

Athena, lovely maiden who wears the aegis true,
We seek again your garment,
To live within its fold,
Content under your skins,
Fringed in radiant gold.

Meditation for Athena

Begin by coming into stillness and releasing all prior occupations of mind and body.

Athena comes to those to possess the mind and might to craft for themselves a life bound in individual freedom that is skillfully woven into the common good. To find her…we must lift our thoughts to the singular radiance and whole harmony of these things.

To find her we must call to mind that which is brave and true within our own nature and the story of our life. Do this now. Remember a time when your life demanded courage and valor; and you, like Odysseus, Jason and Prometheus, were worthy of the guidance and protection of a patroness such as she.

With this memory alive within you…see yourself then…see yourself now…call to mind *your sacred need*. Mindful of your own past bravery and current *sacred need*, sense and see the swift presence of the element of Air.

Air of life swift and clean wrap us in your freedom. Bound not by space or time you flow freely, through all. Air of life carry us deep within the timeless heart of the Earth and to an ancient land called Athens.

Give yourself to these winds wrapping you in pastel breezes while descending into the heart of the Earth beneath you…and then bringing you back upon its surface…outside the Acropolis in Ancient Greece.

Soft winds carry the smells and sounds of the Mediterranean landscape…quiet in this pre-dawn hour. Above you stands a mighty temple of stone with its high walls, softly illuminated by the light of the coming day. Find your way to the steep, stone staircase that marks the East entrance to her temple, where the dimness of night gives way to the warm, golden light of dawn. See the images of Athena's birth cast upon the triangular pediment above this East temple door.

Now look to yourself. See your pilgrim's costume... reminiscent of *your sacred need* ...for you wear upon your skin your own request. You carry within your hands...the tools of your own uncertainty. As any other who comes here...you are transparent to the soft light of her truth.

With all this...begin your ascent up the well-worn steps... listening to the soft sounds of the powdered Earth stirring beneath your feet as you climb...mindful of *your sacred need*. With each step, the Sun also rises...bringing greater and greater light to your walk and your way.

Climb until at last you stand before the eight columns that mark the temple's entrance...beginning to feel her presence upon you, you walk forward but a few steps to meet another six columns that narrow the world toward her.

Coming nearer, a sudden ray of dawning sunlight pierces ahead of you, running deep within the naos, striking the gold clad, ivory skinned body of Athena...suddenly illuminated by the birthing Sun. She stands like a giant among the brightly colored pillars of the past. Beneath her is a still pool, reflecting her image in perfect clarity.

As you walk toward her, past the columns' steadfastness...the breath of life purifies your mind...to truly see her...to truly hear her...to truly know her.

Enter the pool of warm and shallow water before her feet... As the water weights each step with its heaviness you come to stand beneath her towering brilliance...call again to mind your own past valiance…then share with her *your sacred need* of this and the coming time. Commune with Athena, the grey-eyed Goddess of nearness…in silence.

Silence

With this…your time here ends…finish and look about you… following the light of the Sun's eastern rise…walk along its beams that point to the western entrance of the temple. Come to the six columns that open to eight others…come to the eight columns that open to the world beyond. See the western sky illuminated…see the way before you illuminated with her wisdom.

Crossing beyond the temple columns, look above you…to the imagery upon the pediment of the western doorway…see the contest between Athena and Poseidon, and see Athena giving resources and independence to her people.

Now, look again at your own costume and its changes. What resource has she given to you? What tools of Ability have replaced the tools of Need and Uncertainty? Gather close what she has given, as the winds come once again to bundle and carry you into the timeless Earth...blessed with this day's virgin birth all it bestowed…into this room you come again.

With each breath in….and each breath out…fan the bellows of your lungs…until you find yourself alive within your waking consciousness…in full possession of all she's given you... Here …Now.

Sekhmet

Sekhmet

Cultural Origins: Upper Egypt, Memphis & Thebes
Temple Precinct of Mut & Temple of Ptah
Karnak Temple Complex in Luxor
"One Who Is", "Mighty One"

Goddess of: the mid-day Sun, scorching fire, ferocity, fertility and menstruation, deep healing and transformation, love, war, fermentation, physicians and the sacred kingship.

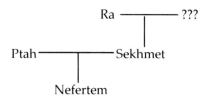

Pantheon & Cultural Mythos: Following the Nile, Ancient Egypt stretched from the Lower Delta through Northern Africa. Its earliest civilizations, dating from approximately 5500 BCE, occurred in the form of small tribes living near the great river. These civilizations grew to become a powerful ancient world culture. Approximately 3200 BCE, the political union of the Upper and Lower Nile codified the social structure of Ancient Egypt under the first pharaoh. It is during this period that the prominence of Sekhmet swelled. The spiritual, material and cultural prosperity of Ancient Egypt continued, through its conquer by Alexander the Great (332 BCE) and until 30 BCE when the Romans subjugated the lands under their domain.

Sekhmet is one of the oldest Goddesses in the greater Egyptian pantheon. In Memphite theology, she is the daughter of the Sun God Ra or Re. No mother is attributed to her. As daughter of the Sun God, she is the feminine embodiment of its fierce, hot, noon-day aspect.

According to Egyptian mythos, Ra became annoyed with humanity, seeing how it failed time and time again to adhere to the rightful ways of law, justice and balance. He decided that punishment was in order, thus he sent his fierce daughter Sekhmet to bring a fearful reckoning to the people. True to her father's command, she brought destruction and dire consequences to the people, many died. Upon seeing this, Ra attempted to disengage Sekhmet, but the heat of her internal Sun was too hot to be quelled with words. To quench her fire and release her from his prior edict, he poured 7,000 gallons of beer and pomegranate juice upon her body, easing her heat-induced fury and ceasing the punishment. She was filled with the beer/pomegranate mixture, became sedate and slept for three days. When she awoke, she was herself again. In one lovely version of this story, upon awakening she sees and falls in love with Ptah, thus beginning their beautiful union.

All cultures fashion punitive myths to help remind themselves that they must act in virtuous ways or suffer the rectification of the Gods/Goddesses. As the embodiment of the most powerful element of the land, the Sun, Sekhmet's fierce presence is warning enough. Those who make the mistake of not truly understanding this story think of her only as a punitive and fearful deity. However, this is only a small aspect of the fullness of her true nature. In our work with her as a *Mother of Change,* it is important that we come to know all of her.

Sekhmet is part of a trinity form: Mother, Father, Child. In this, she is the consort of Ptah, the God of piety; he instills the sacred powers of right speech to the mouth and the heart. Ptah is said to be the architect of the Universe, created by him through the expression of his pure heart and breath. Their child is Nefertem, the God of physicians and perfumes. Together, the triune deities Sekhmet, Ptah and Nefertem embody and impart righteousness, beauty and healing.

Sekhmet has been associated with other Goddesses such as Bast, Hathor, Mut and Wadjet. In contrast to Sekhmet's fierce and fiery nature, her sister Bast, known primarily in Lower Egypt, is the warm, glowing Sun. As Lower Egypt was conquered by Upper Egypt, Sekhmet replaced Bast as the primary Goddess. As Wadjet, the same fiery, protective power manifested in the form of the cobra-Goddess. Wadjet wears the same Sun disk and embodies many of the same qualities as Sekhmet. Sekhmet was a fierce defender of her father, the Sun God; and as such she became an important manifestation of the "Eye of Ra" who devoured the God's enemies. In this aspect she was closely associated with the Goddess Hathor. In Thebes, she was merged with the Goddess Mut, consort of Amun. When Thebes rose to greater prominence, Mut absorbed the warrior Goddesses with many of her aspects.

In Mesopotamian, Mediterranean and Hindu cultures, the lion or tiger and the Goddess are depicted as companions and counterparts (e.g. Inanna, Ishtar and Durga.) In these cultural forms, the Goddess rides or sits upon the lion/tiger. With her lion's head and slim, feminine body, Sekhmet has *merged with* the lion, the two becoming one. Obviously this is an important distinction that separates Sekhmet from other lion/tiger Goddesses.

In all, over 600 statues of Sekhmet were known to exist at the entrance to the Temple of Mut in Karnak (Amenhotep III, 1411-1375 BCE). We know of no other deity whose worship commanded as many representations as Sekhmet. It appears that Amenhotep III's temple, which seems to have fallen into decay quicker than other royal mortuary temples, was a convenient source of ready-made statuary for later kings.

The hot desert wind that arises in Egypt at times was called "the breath of Sekhmet." As the fiery Sun Goddess, Sekhmet is ferocious, but never in an arbitrary manner. She fiercely protects what she loves and that for which she is responsible. Aggression is not initiated by her, but instead offered in response to the righting of a wrong according to her loyalty and her love. In her dangerous aspect, she was said to breathe fire against enemies of the pharaohs. Thus the pharaohs adopted her as their protectress and as a symbol of their own power in battle where they were sometimes said "to rage like Sekhmet." In addition to benefitting her people in war, Sekhmet was also directly associated with the bringing or relieving of pestilence and plague; both were said to be "the messengers of Sekhmet."

In her protective aspect as "Sekhmet, mistress of life," she was called upon as a healing deity. In this capacity, she could be persuaded to remove disease through the administration of special rites called "appeasing Sekhmet" that were performed by her dedicated temple Priests.

In later times, her Priests played important roles in the magical aspect of healing, reciting prayers and spells while the physicians administered physical remedies to the patient. She was also the Goddess called upon during labor and childbirth; in this her strong association to the blood of life and death was of vital importance. This same attribute brought additional distinction to Sekhmet, for she was also the Goddess of menstruation, and as such was endowed with the creative power of the sacred blood of the feminine.

Religious/Spiritual Observations: Priestesses performed rituals to her each day in different representations to bring healing and protection and to stave off pestilence and illness. Her Priests had a working knowledge of the physical heart, which distinguished them in Egyptian society. The Priest's recitation of prayers to Sekhmet was as integral a part of a patient's treatment of illness as was the physician's administering of portions and remedies. To commemorate the prior myth told, each Feast Day of Hathor/Sekhmet called for the drinking of beer stained with pomegranate juice.

Symbols and Attributes: Sun, fierce fire, heat, healing transformation, war, blood of life and fertility, blood of death and destruction, lion-headed Goddess, crowned by the Sun disc with a fire-spitting cobra encircling its perimeter. The color red (as blood) is often associated with her. She holds an ankh and a scepter reminiscent of a papyrus stalk, the heraldic Northern Egyptian plant. She is known by 99 names, often spoken aloud to call upon the fullness of her power and presence. Goddess of the South and the powers of Initiation and Illumination within the body of Archangel Michael.

Sekhmet is a *Mother of Change* because she presides over transformation, especially the thresholds of life and death. She is a fierce healer who purifies and cleanses any and all maladies, bad tendencies or falseness; thus enabling change from within consistent with the demands of the change without.

Incantation to Sekhmet

Sekhmet, Power-filled…Mighty One,
Goddess of the mid-day Sun,
And the midnight chambers' guiding flame.

Of Ra, a Daughter,
Of Nefertem, a Mother,
Of Ptah, a most beloved Queen.

Crowned with Solar flares,
And the serpent's righteous glare,
Of scarlet cloth adorned,
To you, we come forewarned
For in your lion's eyes,
All truth and depth are seen.

Opener of the way,
That heals the venerable,
And destroys the terrible,
Loyal to all who love and who revere.

Initiator….Enlightener…Illuminator
Shining, incomparable Sekhmet,
To you we gift the ruby,
And the rose.

Meditation for Sekhmet

Begin by coming into stillness and releasing all prior occupations of mind and body.

To find her…we must be willing to be fully seen.
To find her…we wish to be transformed from the inside… underneath the skin…underneath the Earth.

With this willingness and wish, remember *your sacred need.*
Bring it to the forefront of your heart and mind in clarity and softness.

Envision her original home in Egypt's Lower Nile Delta. Now, garnering your own fiery will forces, drop a line of consciousness deep into the Earth beneath your feet…continuing this downward motion until you reach the molten core of the planet. Then, allow heat's natural rising force to push you back through the earthen layers below…surfacing again in the Egyptian desert, under a blazing noon-day Sun. See yourself robed in white, protected from the searing heat, walking sandal-footed through the windswept landscape.

Walking forward you see the faint outline of a distant door… simple, rectangular. It is made of sandstone and mortar. As you near this door, details etched upon the stone become clear to you and you know that this is the entrance you seek. The blackness in the center of this open doorway gives no clue as to the mystery beyond its frame. Holding fast to *your sacred need,* place your hands upon the frame of the doorway and make your prayers.

As your petitioning words are spoken, the walls beyond the door are softly illuminated by the sudden flare of two torches. In their luminescence, you see a descending sandstone staircase. As your eyes adjust to the change of light…the smell of temple incense wafts upward to greet you, encouraging your descent. When you feel ready, make your journey down the stairs and into the underground temple.

At the end of your descent, you find yourself standing in a simple room also lit by wall hung torches. The coolness of the underground chamber relieves of you the Sun's burden and once again, your eyes adjust to the changed light.

Coming to you now are the guardians of this temple, one a Priest, the other a Priestess. They meet you with a silent gaze that fills you with a peaceful understanding of their purpose. Soon, you begin walking together toward an adjacent chamber.

As your sight sharpens, you see the chamber and its occupant resting regally in the center where a large stone altar holds the reclined sarcophagus of the God Ptah. With the surety of your own knowing, walk toward the ornate casket, adorned with gold, rubies and sapphires. Stand, steady at the feet of Ptah and be still.

It is Ptah who prepares you for Sekhmet…it is he who takes upon his breath all that is physical within you…leaving you with the energy bodies that connect you to the subtle realms.

Place your hands upon his feet and open your mouth. Feel the great winds of the underground stir around you as Ptah inhales into himself all the solid matter of your physical body...leaving you, in a pure form of energy alone.

With this, the Priest comes to your right and the Priestess your left…to uphold you. Give yourself to them, as they lift and guide your subtle nature away from Ptah's sarcophagus and through the chamber door…and into another hall.

Prepared...you come now to her chamber door beyond which ruby colored walls glow with the golden hew of flaming sconces, that warm even the deep underground chamber with her fire.

See before you, the body of the lion-headed Goddess, carved in black basalt. She stands sure and tall; crowned with the golden Solar disk and coiled cobra. In her right hand, she holds the key of life; in her left hand the lotus wand…she extends one foot outward, as if she would come toward you.

Looking upon her face, her silver eyes seem to stare through you…in a moment you are "known to her." Receive…match… and let nothing break this gaze, remain steady…in her presence…in silence…and be very still.

With her permission, her Priest and Priestess now escort you through the doorway and toward her…placing your inner being on the ground before her, then they turn and walk away, leaving you with her.

Be awake… be quiet…and watch…as Sekhmet opens the way, healing the venerable within you, destroying the terrible within you, readying you for the changes according to *your sacred need*…in silence.

Silence

With this, a Priest and Priestess of Sekhmet come again to your right and left to uphold and guide you back through her chamber door…and into the hall.

Gently they lead you back to the chamber and feet of Ptah…be still.

When you are ready, place your hands upon his feet and open your mouth. Feel the great winds of the underground stir around you, as Ptah exhales all the solid matter of your physical body...back unto you. Be still as the mass and might of you come together again as one. Sense the changes working within you as your subtle and physical natures re-entwine.

When this integration is complete, breathe in and out...then escorted by the Priest and Priestess, make your way back to the landing at the foot of the stairs that gave you entrance to this underground temple.

As they look upon you one final time and prepare you for your exit, they may touch your physical body, sealing this experience. Receive this touch in confidence and trust.

With this, make your way back up the stairs...and into the hot noon-day desert land.

Standing still, envision again a line of consciousness permeating the world beneath your feet...follow this line of light to the center of the Earth. And again, ride the force of rising heat to gently ascend back to the surface and the place where your physical body rests now.

With each breath in....and each breath out...fan the bellows of your lungs...until you find yourself alive within your waking consciousness...in full possession of all she's given you... Here...Now.

Miryam

Miryam

Cultural Origins: Judeo-Christian & Muslim
Mother of Yeshua ben Joseph or Jesus
Priestess from Davidic Line of Nazareth
Miryam – transliteration from Aramaic "Mapia" or "Mapiay"

Mother of: grace, mercy, love and compassion; Yeshua ben Joseph or Jesus Christ, one of devotion and commitment to Divine purpose and the ways of the sacred initiation.

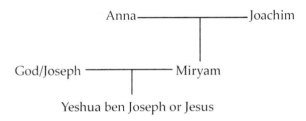

Pantheon & Cultural Mythos: Miryam, as mother of Jesus, is mentioned in the Gospels of Matthew (1:16, 18-25) and Luke 1:26-56, 2:1-7 in the New Testament of the Christian Bible. In Matthew, the most humble of references is given to her as a woman who is with child before her marriage. Her husband is about to divorce her for her obvious betrayal, but an angel of the Lord tells Joseph that Miryam's child is holy and he should not abandon her.

In Luke, we receive more information. Luke starts by setting the historical context for Yeshua's birth telling us that there was a Priest named Zacharias (or Zachariah), of the division of Abijah[3], under the rule of King Herod the Great.[4] Zacharias and his wife Elizabeth were without child. One day, Zacharias (who was a devoted and holy man) entered the temple to light the incense, as was his duty, when an angel appeared before him announcing the pregnancy of his Elizabeth with a son to be called John (John the Baptist). In the sixth month of Elizabeth's pregnancy, God sent another angel, Gabriel, to Nazareth to a virgin named Miryam betrothed to a man named Joseph, of the House of David. During this visitation, Gabriel told Miryam that she had found favor with God and would conceive in her womb a son to be called Jesus. The angel foretold of the greatness of her son and his deeds.

The Gospel of Luke goes on to say that after receiving this news, Miryam journeyed to stay with Elizabeth for three months before returning home. During the initial moments of her arrival at Elizabeth and Zacharias' home, the baby in Elizabeth's womb leapt, filling its mother with the Holy Spirit and thus she spoke, "Blessed art thou among women and blessed is the fruit of thy womb." (Luke 1: 40-42)

Just prior Miryam's time of delivery; Caesar Augustus decreed that all people must take part in a taxation census, requiring all citizens to return to their home city to be counted. As Joseph's home was Bethlehem, he and Miryam journeyed there to be counted. While in Bethlehem, Miryam entered labor, and as there was no room in the inn, she gave birth in a simple, wooden manger. This story is all we receive of Miryam from the Gospel of Luke.

In the assertions of the Eastern Orthodox, Ethiopian/Coptic and Greek Orthodox churches we are told a great deal more about Miryam, as the following excerpt extracted from the Archbishop Dmitri of Dallas and The South states:

> "The Orthodox Church honors and venerates the Virgin Mary as "more honourable than the Cherubim and more glorious without compare than the Seraphim." Her name is mentioned in every service, and her intercession before the throne of God is asked. She is given the title of "Theotokos" (Greek for "Birth-giver-of-God), as well as "Mother of God". She has a definite role in Orthodox Christianity, and can in no way be considered an instrument which, once

used, was laid aside and forgotten. Objections to the veneration of the Theotokos are based primarily on what is called "a lack of scriptural evidence to support such a practice." While it is true that the Church depends heavily on her Tradition other than Holy Scripture (Ecumenical Councils, liturgical books, and the writings of the Fathers) for details and the precise definition of the nature of the veneration of the Virgin Mary, there are several passages of the New Testament that really form the basis for our practice." [5]

In the Orthodox teachings, we learn Miryam's parents were named Anna (of Bethlehem) and Joachim[6] (of Nazareth[7]). Though they were devout people, dedicated faithfully to their temple, Joachim and Anna's twenty-year marriage was childless. So concerned were they on this account, that they promised if they would be blessed with child, it would be devoted to the service of God.

One fateful day, the temple Priest publically chastised Joachim for his childlessness marriage, casting great shame upon him and his wife, Anna. However, soon after this difficult admonishment, an angel appeared to Joachim announcing the birth of a daughter who was to be called Miryam and, according to their promise, bequeathed to the temple at age three. The angel also told him that while Miryam was yet a virgin, she would bear and bring forth the Son of God. Joachim was further instructed that Miryam was not to eat unclean foods or converse with common people, thus ensuring her safety from unwarranted slander or suspicion. Soon after, the angel appeared to Anna with the same announcement.

As decreed, Anna and Joachim did indeed conceive a child. When Miryam was three years old, she was given to the women's court in the temple. While there, she created beautiful tapestries and cloths while receiving the teachings given to women. It is understood that the temple to which Miryam was dedicated was, among other things, a Temple of the Moon, the element of Water and the cycles of fertility. As the Jewish calendar is Lunisolar (i.e. indicating both the Moon phase and the time of the Solar year,) this is not wholly surprising.

Temple virgins reached the end of their service at age twelve, prior to their first blood; which, if occurring within the temple would be a source of pollution. Thus just before their coming of age, the High Priest betrothed his temple virgins to prominent men in the community. It is said that Miryam refused marriage saying her place was within the temple, and in service to God. This greatly concerned the High Priest for he knew she could not stay. In an attempt to solve this problem with the sensitivity due to her, the High Priest commanded a meeting of the temple's head men. All came together to request Divine guidance upon the betrothal of Miryam. During their contemplation, a divination-based test was given to the High Priest. He was told he must administer this test to find the true husband of Miryam. According to the guidance, the High Priest was to ask all unmarried men of the House of David to bring their staffs to the altar in the temple. The staff that flowered would indicate the one who was to be betrothed to the reluctant virgin.

Joseph, who was advanced in years, felt uncomfortable standing with the younger men for this honor. Thus, he held his staff back when others presented theirs. As a result, in the initial test no man's staff flowered. Seeing this, the High Priest declared that someone must be withholding their staff as the test was purely given, and thus all would present again. With this Joseph relinquished and presented his staff along with the others. When he did, a dove descended from the temple's dome and perched upon it, signaling he was to be Miryam's husband.

Having received the news, Miryam journeyed to her parent's home to prepare for the wedding ceremonies. Joseph journeyed to his family's abode to do the same. It is said that while in their respective homes, the angel Gabriel came to speak to them both as was told in the New Testament writings previously referenced.

In the apocryphal text, *The Protovangelion of James*, believed to have been written by James the lesser, cousin and brother of Jesus, a similar tale of Miryam's birth and destiny is told. In this version of the story, Joachim was a rich man who made extra offerings to God in hopes of benefiting his people and receiving forgiveness for his sins.[8] One day as he made his offerings, the High Priest spoke out, admonishing Joachim for being the only man in their temple who had not fathered a child for the tribe. Shamed and alarmed, Joachim consulted the registries to see if he did indeed deserve the Priest's admonishment. Sadly, he found the accusation to be true. In despair, he retired to the wilderness fasting and praying for forty days. During this time, Anna mourned her barrenness alone. However, one day in her grieving, Anna perceived that a sparrow in a laurel tree bemoaning her barrenness. In that moment, an angel appeared to her and told her she would conceive. The rest of the story follows the prior Orthodox version until we come to Miryam's own pregnancy.

Miryam is committed to Joseph via the High Priests' prior divined determination and the long, many-celebrations wedding, then observed in Judaism, began. The marriage rites were only partly complete when Joseph learned that his work required him to leave for six months. One day during his absence, Miryam was drawing a pot of water at the well when she heard a voice that caused her to tremble. Just then, an angel appeared to her, foretelling her of the Divine conception to come. As before, she visits Elizabeth soon after receiving this news.

Joseph returns from building houses to find Miryam six months pregnant. Knowing the child cannot be his, he reproaches her. She affirms her innocence. That night in his sleep, an angel comes to Joseph in a dream warning him to reverse his judgment of Miryam.

Anna also visits Miryam, and seeing her pregnant, assumes that Joseph and she married outside the final temple rites. This breech of Jewish law must be conveyed to the Priest; and thus reluctantly she had to do so. Knowing they will be brought to trial on the charge, Miryam and Joseph decide to leave together.

When Miryam nears her time to deliver, Joseph places her safely in a nearby cave and leaves to find a proper midwife. During his search, he perceives many strange signatures in nature which guide him onward. Soon he finds a midwife; however as they arrive at the cave where Miryam labors, the midwife questions him as to the legitimacy of this child. Just then, a great light surrounds the cave and the baby is born. The midwife tells her friend Salome of this miraculous birth. Salome comes to see the child, and upon touching him, proclaims him to be a great king. Wise men also come to the cave to visit the baby. These attentions paid, soon find and alarm King Herod. With warning, the new family is advised to leave Bethlehem secretly, and thus avoid the jealous King's wrath.

It has often been said that Miryam is mentioned more in the Qur'ān than in the entire New Testament of the Christian Bible; this depends upon your point of reference.

Chapter Nineteen of the Qur'ān is called *Maryam* (based upon her Syriac name.) When we read the English translations of the Qur'ān, we find here a description of the child given to Zacharias and Elizabeth. From there it moves to discuss the sacredness of Miryam, including the annunciation. It is true that the Qur'ān's description of the visitation of angel Gabriel is much more detailed than that of the New Testament. However, once this story is relayed, the text moves away from Miryam for the duration of the chapter.

The Qur'ān shares the *Protovangelion's* emphasis on Miryam's purity, prayerfulness and perseverance. She is also honored for withstanding adversity in the face of great hardship. Tim Winter's helpful essay *Mary in Islam*, included in the Oxford Press publication *Mary: The Complete Resource*[9] adds to our understanding of Miryam's place in Islam:

> *"Mary is a figure of very slight relevance, offering a scriptural basis for the belief in the miracles of the saints, but little more. Rather more significant was Mary's importance for historians and authors of Qur'ān commentaries, who assembled extensive anecdotes about Mary, the exact ancestry of most of which cannot now be determined.*
>
> *In popular culture, and in mysticism, both sophisticated and rustic, the drama and prayerfulness of the Qur'ānic story generated a Marian culture of considerable richness."*

Winter goes on to say that it is of course Fātima, the Prophet's daughter, who rivals Miryam as the other perfect woman, and thus an example for Muslim women to follow. In truth, Miryam's unrepeatable miracle (the virgin birth), negates her as a truly helpful model for Muslim women to emulate.

Religious/Spiritual Observations: Miryam has always been revered, both prior to and since the advent of Christianity. In the Orthodox/Gnostic/Essene and Catholic faiths, she is honored as "Theotokos," the Mother of God. She is bequeathed nineteen holy days of feast and prayer within the Liturgical Calendar. In the Protestant faiths she is loved, but not worshiped according to Luther's dictates. Muslims honor her as the mother of an important Prophet.

Symbols & Attributes: Lunar emblems, water, wells, love, compassion, giving and receiving, the Moon, the Madonna Lily that blooms during the observed time of the Assumption.

She is often seen clothed in blue standing upon the Moon with her head in a crown of twelve Stars. Goddess of the West and the powers of Love and Compassion within the body of Archangel Gabriel.

Miryam is a *Mother of Change* because she was bound by the change that her womb would offer the world. Not only did she birth the beginning of a whole new era, she was prepared from the age of three for this great task. Her entire life was dedicated and devoted to the change she was to bear as well as the pain and difficulty that same change would bring upon her.

Incantation to Miryam

Miryam,
Blessed one of temple and of truth,
Whose womb would bear the fruit of love,
Whose eyes would see the pain of love,
And the glorious light of love renewed.

Virgin of blood and of spirit,
Of water's own purity,
Gather us into your lunar cup.

Until we see with eyes of love,
Until we speak with tongues of love,
Engulfed in love's unending spirit up.

Unto your dusk-drawn day,
Our souls we do convey,
And promise to uphold the vision true.

That your own rich blood be known,
Beyond the bishop's throne,
With us,
And with the rest,
As is your due.

Meditation for Miryam

Begin by coming into stillness and releasing all prior occupations of mind and body.

To find her, we must let go of all preconceptions we have of the woman called Mary, Maria, Miryam as humble servant and unwitting virgin…placid and innocent.

To find her…we must see instead a blue-robed Priestess of the oceanic Temple of the West ruled by the Moon. As an agent of the Archangel Gabriel, the messenger of souls and fertility, she mediates love and compassion from the spirit world into the world of form. Her virginal nature is that of pure streams of a royal bloodline and enlightened consciousness simultaneously embodied.

With this understanding alive within you…call to mind *your sacred need*. Call it clearly to you. As you do…see a whirling pool of bright water swell beneath your feet in a swift and circular motion…watch as the soils open to its currents, taking it and you deep within the heart of the timeless Earth…into the Earth…into its core and up again, rising with the waters' swell…ascending back to the surface…standing in the shallow, lapping currents on the shore of the Sea of Galilee.

See before you the landscape of her life…and the setting Sun at dusk. Soft evening winds cool your skin as the sky continues to deepen into a living mural of pink, orange, blue, gold and indigo.

Stand within the water's gentle sway, feel their kiss upon your feet as the sands shift and change beneath you with the tide's ebb and flow. Hold fast to *your sacred need*…and wait….wait with all sincerity for Miryam, Priestess of the Temple of the

West, wait as the dimly lit Moon begins to rise in the darkening sky.

With sincerity's promise, in the periphery of your vision you see her coming toward you; walking calmly along the shoreline, cloaked in beautiful robes of blue. Her pace is sure and gentle... purposeful and peaceful…as she makes her way along the water's edge to where you stand.

Seeing, as no other sees, she comes to stand before you, staring into your eyes. She takes her place within the slightly deeper sea between you and the Moon kissed waters beyond. Look…look into the eyes of Miryam of Nazareth, for the very first time. See all you've never known about her.

This once human woman knows what it is be tried and tested to the core of our being. This once human woman knows what it is live in times of great change. She offers herself, her love and compassion to you in the simple and direct manner of a gaze.

The Moon's brilliant silver rays stream through her…in a moment everything changes as the power of Luna Oceana is mediated through Miryam and into you. Commune with this power in response to *your sacred need* in a moment of silence.

Watch as she steps toward you bringing the palms of her hands together in front of her heart as if to pray; yet no prayers leave her lips. Instead her hands are filled with a light that is both powerful and gentle....radiant and still.

According to *your sacred need*, the light in Miryam's hands come to rest upon you now…filling you with the power of love and compassion…in just the right measure...in just the right way. Be still…and know that she is one with the ocean and Moon… and the power of love and compassion.

Silence

With this gift deeply seeded within you now, Miryam folds her hands back upon her breast, withdrawing her touch, but not her eyes' gaze upon you. Still her beautiful eyes press open your heart…to receive and remember…all taken…and all given…by her touch…the touch of The Ancient Ones.

After a moment's pregnant pause, she lifts her gaze from your eyes and withdraws into herself again. Gently she turns and begins her journey back along the sea shore and into the distance. Soon…she fades into the dim evening light.

The gathering waters are stirred again around your feet…these whirling waters slowly take you back into the heart of the timeless Earth. See yourself rising up again…upon the water's swift currents to this space and place.

With each breath in….and each breath out…fan the bellows of your lungs…until you find yourself alive again within your waking consciousness…in full possession of all she's given you... Here…Now.

Inanna

Inanna

Cultural Origins: Sumeria 4000-2900 BCE
Uruk Period, Lower Tigris & Euphrates River Settlement
Nin (lady) An (sky) Ninna (owl)

Goddess of: love and war, fertility and destruction, lightening that catalyzes fire and the extinguishing of fires, tears and rejoicing, Queen of Heaven and Earth, Goddess of the Morning & Evening Star; maker of kings, sacred prostitute, sacred sexuality, Lunar Goddess.

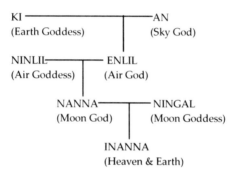

Pantheon & Cultural Mythos: Sumer (pronounced shoomer) was located in modern day Iraq (roughly Baghdad near the Persian Gulf) and is thought to be one of the earliest civilizations in the world dating back to 6000 BCE, at least. Sumerians, themselves are said to come from a distant culture, likely somewhere in south-central Asia. They referred to themselves as ùĝ saĝ gíg-ga, phonetically *uŋ saŋ giga*, literally meaning "the black -headed people."

The Sumerians believed that the ocean surrounded the Universe on all sides; therefore the deep sea was the source of all life. This reinforces the understanding (held by some) that the Sumerian culture was one of the seed-bearing cultures of Atlantis; post the deluge that destroyed it. The following information helps paint a picture of this dignified, regal and intelligent culture that greatly impacted the growth and progression of human society in general.

Sumer was itself a collection of over a dozen city-states all defined by their own agricultural systems and temples, each with resident Gods and Goddesses as protectors. The people, the city and all belongings were considered the property of the patron God or Goddess.

Like many early cultures, the Sumerians lived in a class-based social structure ranging from nobles to slaves. Marriages were arranged by parents who sought prosperity for and longevity of the family line. Interestingly, where many older cultures restricted the rights of women, in Sumer they had many significant privileges; among them were the rights to hold property and engage in business.

Sumer was a dry and hot land with little initial promise. However its people were gifted, energetic and innovative. Employing their ingenuity and the rhythms of their Lunar calendar, they were the first to practice annual agriculture using complex irrigation and food storage regimes (circa 5300 BCE.) Pottery and reed baskets were used for storage. Fire places and fire altars were found in homes and temple buildings. Copper, gold and silver were incorporated into their tools, arts and adornments. Instrumental and vocal music was important in Sumerian life, as were artisans and craftsmen. It is important to note that writing was developed in this culture around 3500 BCE, moving humanity from hieroglyphic to cuneiform tablet communication and preservation.

Inanna's worship emerged in the Uruk period of Sumerian history, between 4000-2900 BCE. Evidence of her worship spanned some 3000 years from its earliest to latest archeological representations. She was the Sumerian's Queen of Heaven, as the Morning and Evening Star and of Earth in the fertility of the lands. The follow excerpts taken from Diane Wolkstein and Samuel Noah Kramer's well-noted book *Inanna: Queen of Heaven and Earth, Her Stories and Hymns from Sumer"*[10] provide a beautiful and poetic account of her place among those who revered her, as translated from the original cuneiform.

> *"The people of Sumer parade before you.*
> *They play the sweet ala-drums before you.*
> *The people of Sumer parade before you.*
> *I say "Hail!" to Inanna, Great Lady of Heaven!*
>
> *They beat the holy drum and timpani before you.*
> *The people of Sumer parade before you.*
> *I say "Hail" to Inanna, First Daughter of the Moon!*
>
> *The male prostitutes comb their hair before you.*
> *They decorate the napes of their necks with colored scarves,*
> *They drape the cloak of the Gods about their shoulders.*
> *The righteous men and women walk before you.*
> *They hold the soothing harp by their sides.*
> *Those who follow wear the sword belt.*
> *They grasp the spear in their hands.*
> *They carry the sword and the double-edged ax.*
>
> *The Priest, who covers his sword with blood, sprinkles blood,*
> *He sprinkles blood over the throne of the court chamber.*
> *In the Heavens the Holy One appears alone (saying).*
> *My Lady looks in sweet wonder from Heaven.*
> *She looks in sweet wonder on all the lands.*
> *And on the people of Sumer as numerous as sheep."*

Inanna was everything to her people; in fact few old world Mother Goddesses encompassed as much in their embrace. In her capacity as Queen of Heaven and Earth, she provided for all aspects of human and agricultural fertility, ranging from the practical aspects of plowing the fields to the sensual aspects of human love-making. The poetry dedicated to Inanna combines her human and natural benevolence in a manner that is sacred, erotic and thoroughly invigorating to the senses. As she who initiates and quells, Inanna gives and takes in many forms including love and hate, peace and war, fertility and barrenness, rejoicing and tears. In this we see that she embodies the harsh reality of a life sculpted by the forces of the ever-present and co-mingled spiritual powers of the "opposites."

As Queen of Heaven and Earth, she felt compelled to journey to the Underworld. In her famous descent, Inanna meets, offends and then receives the blessings of her dark sister Ereshkigal, Queen of the Underworld. Through this great endeavor she assumes the powers of life, death and the transformation. This feat secured her position as the Lunar Goddess and she who ruled over all phases of Sumerian life and death. In this context, I feel it is important to correct a common misunderstanding attributed to Ereshkigal assigned, I believe, by a psychological approach erroneously applied to her mythos.

In Sumerian folklore, the primary function the dark Goddess Ereshkigal was to weep over the deaths of children. This was a distinct and important occupation for the people of this culture for, according to their beliefs, the life a person led on the surface world did not determine the conditions of the afterlife. Instead the quality of the afterlife was determined by the way people cared for the dead in the days following their passing: great mourning equaled great afterlife honors. Ereshkigal's sacred task of weeping for the dead children of Sumer would have been a great service to their soul's journeys and the quality of their afterlife. Thus when the kurgarra, fashioned by Inanna's father Enki to aid Inanna's rescue, moaned and groaned in commiseration with Ereshkigal, she said: "If you are Gods, I will bless you. If you are mortals I will give you a gift." Thus they retrieved and revived the body of Inanna.

By voluntarily descending into the Underworld as she did, Inanna assumed some of the powers Ereshkigal had carried solely before. This also served to increase Inanna's spiritual capacity as being a Mother Goddess of opposing forces.

The growing salinity of the soils and the rising Tigris and Euphrates river beds caused a northward migration of the Sumerian culture. As with many of the ancient Mother Goddesses, Inanna's worship faded with the introduction of the patriarchal lineage and the rise in the worship of Marduk. Inanna did, however, resurface again in the northern Babylonian and Assyrian cultures as Ishtar. As Ishtar, her attributes were expanded to include guardian of law, shepardess of lands, forgiver of sins and righteous judge. These qualities further align Inanna with the symbols and attributes of the North/Earth and her unique place within *The Mothers of Change*.

Religious/Spiritual Observations: The Sumerian temples were a repository of the grains and accumulated wealth of the people. As such, they were fiercely guarded by their patron Gods and Goddesses. The form known to us as the Ziggurat was their design, which can be traced back to the Atlantean Fire Temples of some 4,000 years prior. The Ziggurat is shaped in progressively decreasing levels, wide on the bottom and narrow on the top. It is believed that the Zoroastrian Fire Temples were inherited from the Sumerian designs.

Sumerians (and Babylonians later) boasted a class of citizenry called Astronomer Priests who were well-skilled in the arts of astrology/astronomy and all these disciplines could offer their civilization. Commensurate with the rise and fall of the Morning & Evening Star, that is Venus, offerings were made to Inanna in the morning and the evening by the sacred prostitutes in her temple. Public rites and rituals played a dominant role in Sumerian religion, the most important of which was the annual New Year celebration of the sacred marriage rite of love and procreation.

Symbols & Attributes: rosette, Venus: the eight-pointed Star, lion, ram, hook-shaped and twisted reeds representing the doorpost of the storehouse, opposing Cosmic forces intertwining and inseparable. Goddess of the North and the powers of Destruction and Regeneration within the body of Archangel Auriel.

Inanna is a *Mother of Change* **because** her Lunar, Stellar and Underworld mythos speaks to the inner mysteries of death and transformation. Inanna was worshiped during a time of great cultural change commensurate with the transition from a nomadic to a settled way of life. She is a Goddess of opposites; whose powers mirror those found in the North/Earth, namely Destruction, Regeneration and Cosmic Law.

Incantation to Inanna

Inanna, we call to you,
Through night skies of lapis blue,
Queen of Heaven,
Queen of Earth,
Beloved one of noble birth.

Clad in royal garments of the holy me,
Beloved as none other,
to whom Gods have given sway.

Goddess of Love…Matron of War,
Before you holy drums beat,
and sweet lyres swell with sacred song,
Behind you the severing sword,
and double-axe of justice swings.

Lady of the Morning and Evening Star,
Gaze upon us with glistening eyes,
in our times of darkness.

And when we forget the truth of our Unity,
Lost in our dry and arid controversies,
May the river banks burst forth,
with the flood-waves of your Mercy.

Meditation for Inanna

Begin by coming into stillness and releasing all prior occupations of mind and body.

To find her...we must open ourselves to the cardinal patterning of love and war...life and death.

To find her...we must call to the primal and sensual song lines of light and dark...knowing and unknowing deep within us...and within all of humanity.

This cardinal patterning…these primal and sensual song lines are enfolded into the layers of the Earth...layers of cities made and cities crumbled...of bone and blood...of beauty and of hatred...of old life's decay and new life's springing forth.
Give yourself to this other way...of light and dark forever comingled...within you...and beyond you in the world of nature. And in this, recall *your sacred need*. Place it firmly within your mind and heart.

Come now again, to the sacred will that you possess...use this will to burrow deep into the timeless Earth deep beneath your feet... going into its core...and now rise again through dark matter and luminosity...to the surface and to an ancient land today called Iraq; known before as Sumer...Sumer at midnight.

Indigo skies surround you, filled with the sounds and smells of midnight...vitality at midnight. Crickets chirp in incessant ebbs and swells, night hunting owls call to one another high within the huluppu trees. Just above their canopy, you see a sky adorned with innumerable Stars. The fertility of this land fills your nose as night-blooming flowers cast their perfumes into the winds that gently caress your skin.

Filled by all these sights, sound and smells...look now toward the city walls and the Sun-bleached temple standing proudly at the mouth of the great rivers. See how it is illuminated with oil-filled cauldrons set aflame. Though this Star does not shine above us at midnight, you feel Venus, the Morning and Evening Star, burning under the Earth, far beneath your feet, slowly making its way to the morning sky of tomorrow.

Sounds and smells swell even more, coaxing you away from your standing place and toward the distant temple's sacred flames.

Walk softly into this vital night absorbing all that surrounds you, until you come to the steep and winding stairs of the temple harbor. Hold fast to *your sacred need* and begin your slow ascent up these steps.

When you crest the stairs, the cauldrons' flames light the facade of the temple's outer walls ornamented with beautiful reliefs of all her temple Priests and the prosperity of her land...see these figures illuminated in the flickering flames.

Near where you stand, an open door invites you closer to her. Standing in its frame now, you gaze into the vast temple across the threshold where torches mounted on the walls illuminate all within. This great room is lined with tall clay jars filled with olive oil and rounded baskets holding precious grains. These stores sit heavy upon the temple floor carpeted with woven grass mats.

In the center of the hall, a small pool rises off the ground, filled with green reeds and lotus blossoms. The life it nourishes fills the great hall with an exquisite perfume.

Passing through the center of the temple, your eye soon finds the furthest wall and the massive figure of its protectress, Inanna, carved in relief, gracefully upon it.

Adorned in the holy me, Inanna stands clad in all her finery, accompanied by her owl and ram, her hook and woven reeds and the Morning and Evening Star, her Venus.

As you near the great mural carving...the polarities within you come alive...light and dark...love and hate... creativity and destruction...tears and rejoicing. Feel her presence stir the opposites within you...as she assesses that within you which must be destroyed...and that within you which may be preserved...in response to *your sacred need.*

Stand physically still and silent...encased within her power and her knowing. Stand perfectly still as she gives and takes, destroys and preserves according to *your sacred need.*

Silence

With this...your time here closes. Making your peace with all that has occurred, according to *your sacred need,* walk gently back toward the watery pool in the center of the great room. As you arrive at its edge, take a moment to bend down and gaze into the still waters to see your true reflection...gaze at the *true* reflection that she offers you now.

When you've seen your true reflection, scoop this water's mercy into your hands and mouth. Drink deeply of these merciful waters, then stand and turn, making your way back toward the temple's open door.

Down the stairs and into the night....where all the sights and sounds of the vitality of midnight meet you just as they did before. The night pulls you forward, and slowly you come away from the temple and its surroundings.

Standing still upon these arid grounds, engage your will and focus to journey back into the core of the Earth beneath your feet...and up again into this place, the room where you are now...in full possession of all she's given you...Here…Now.

Anankê

Anankê

Cultural Origins: Ancient Greece 9th-6th Centuries BCE
Supernal Weaver Goddess of the Cosmos
"She Who Dwells Atop Creation"
Also known as Anance, Necessity, Anakgh and Necessitas
"Her might permits no resistance" ~ Aeschylus

Goddess of force, constraint, necessity. Mother of the Moirai (meaning "shares or allotted portions") also known as The Three Fates: Atropos, Lachesis and Clotho. An incorporeal, serpentine being whose outstretched arms encompass the whole Cosmos.

Cultural Context & Mythos: Anankê is the primeval Goddess of compulsion or necessity. She emerged fully formed at the very beginning of time. She is mentioned in several Greek texts including those written by Aeschylus, Empedocles, Herodotus and Plato. The following extracts demonstrate the manner in which she was revered by the Ancient Greeks.

> *"I [Prometheus] must bear my allotted doom [to be chained to a mountain] as lightly as I can, knowing that the might of Necessity (Anankê) permits no resistance."*
>
> Aeschylus, *Prometheus Bound*

> *"There is a law of stern Ananke (Necessity), the immemorial ordinance of the gods made fast forever, bravely sworn and sealed."*
>
> Empedocles, poetic fragments

> *"Then, I said, let us begin and create in idea a State; and yet the true creator is necessity, who is the mother of our invention."*
>
> Plato, Republic, Book II

It is said that Anankê and Khronos created order in the Cosmos by becoming intertwined as Fate and Time, driving the rotation of the Heavens. Together they surrounded the great egg of Cosmic creation. As they constricted their coiling, all parts of the manifest world burst forth. On her own, she is the Weaver Goddess of the Heavens who holds an adamantine (of diamond-like luster) spindle between her knees in the classic spinner's pose. The spindle has eight rings or concentric circles/orbits. Above each ring stands a siren uttering one sound. In perfect harmony, all eight sirens' sounds create a single melody or octave, encompassing the sounds of the:

1. Stars	2. Saturn	3. Jupiter	4. Mars
5. Mercury	6.Venus	7. Sun	8. Moon

According to Plato, "the spindle of Necessity is shaped like the ones we know." In other words, it was the same as the standard Greek spindle. It consisted of three parts: a hook, shaft and whorl. As the Weaver Goddess of the Heavens, her spindle encompasses the Solar System in which we live. Anankê gifts us what we "must do" for our soul's growth; she is the Goddess of necessity. In this, she casts the arrangement of the Stars and Planets at our birth, thus creating our natal chart. Her three daughters, Clotho, Atropos and Lachesis, aid their mother in determining the make and measure of us all.

In Plato's *Republic, Book X, The Myth of Er,* a rich tale of Anankê (as Necessity) is told. Here a young warrior, injured on the battlefield, lies in a coma among many dead comrades. Fueled by the power of their transition *en masse,* he begins the afterlife journey with them, but as he is not dead, he does not complete it. Through this experience, he learns and returns with the knowledge of all that occurs between one life and the next. As she who presides over the necessity and choice of each life we live, Anankê features prominently in the *Myth of Er.* Prior to each incarnation, we visit Anankê. It is here that the destiny (or necessity) and pattern (or choice) of our lives is determined by the casting, and choosing, of lots. To begin, her herald casts tiles at the feet of our soul. In this, our destiny is determined by the tile that lands nearest to us…and thus is "by necessity" given as that which must be done. Then the herald scatters a second set of tiles that hold the many patterns of a life. It is from these tiles that we must choose "how" we will live the destiny bequeathed to us by Anankê.

While Anankê chooses our destiny, we choose "how" we live it. Choosing the pattern presents the supreme hazard for man, and the place where our application is needed. Here we learn (though the course of our many lives) how to distinguish life choices that are good and honorable from life choices that are not. Plato's herald completes his duties by reminding us that virtue comes to us more or less according to our honoring or dishonoring her, in this, the Divine is blameless; we choose for ourselves.

After choosing the life pattern, our soul is marshaled before Lachesis (literally, "disposer of lots"). It is she that binds us to the guardian spirits who help us fulfill our life's purpose and choice. From here we are led to Clotho (literally, "spinner") who ratifies our destiny and chosen pattern, and then finally to Atropos (literally "without turning") who makes the web of our destiny and chosen pattern irreversible.

Once acted upon by the three daughters of Anankê, we pass underneath her throne. From here we journey toward the Earth and embodiment. To do so, we must first cross the long, hot Plain of Oblivion. Tired and thirsty, we come to the River of Forgetfulness where we are required to drink a measure of the waters. Those of us not saved by our good sense drink equal to our thirst and thus forget a great deal of our destiny and choice. Those of us that are wise, drink not according to our thirst and thus retain some of the memory of our destiny and choice. With this, at once our soul falls asleep, descending to Earth like a shooting Star, awakening into our own birth.

Religious/Spiritual Observations: Pausanias was a Greek geographer and traveler who lived in the second century. In his famous first-hand account called *Description of Greece* the following is said which gives us some sense of the religious/spiritual observations of Anankê in Corinth, prior to the Orphic mystery religions which supplanted the older traditions of Ancient Greece.

> *"The Akrokorinthos [at Korinthos or Corinith] is a mountain peak above the city, assigned to Helios by Briareos when he acted as adjudicator [i.e. between Helios and Poseidon in their contest for Korinthos], and handed over, the Korinthians say, by Helios to Aphrodite. As you go up this Akrokorinthos you see two precincts of Isis, one is Isis, surnamed Pelagin (Marine,) and the other of Egyptian Isis, and two of Serapis, one of them being of Serapis called Of Kanopos. After these are altars to Helios, and a sanctuary of Ananke (Necessity) and Bia (Goddess of Force), into which it is not customary to enter."*

Symbols & Attributes: The spindle, the Solar System, the natal chart, destiny and choice, the knees of night, her three daughters of fate: Clotho, Atropos and Lachesis. Later in Roman mythology she was Necessitas who was said to carry "brazen nails" with which she fixed the degrees of fate (natal chart.)

Anankê is a *Mother of Change* because it is she who sets the pattern of necessity for each and every life we live. She sets the patterns and positions of our natal chart, which will both challenge and empower us in a life. In other words, it is she who sculpts us *for the times* in which we live…complete with things to learn and gifts to offer.

Incantation to Anankê

The spindle of creation,
Vast within the Heavens,
Turns between the knees of Anankê.

Its shaft so tall,
It soars through all,
That Time records alone.

The hook and curl,
The face-carved whorl,
Knows all,
As it has been and will ever be.
While ring, within ring
Eight sirens sing,
An ancient celestial reverie.

To answer the calling,
A soul's Star falling,
Back toward the Earth again.

As Lachesis sends the spirits...chosen,
Clotho spins the cloth....handwoven,
And Atropos the dewy threads doth seal.

Over pass...and under Throne,
A weary soul journeys on,
Forgetting...and remembering still.

Meditation for Anankê

Begin by coming into stillness and releasing all prior occupations of mind and body.

Anankê comes to those who seek to remember true, all that was given and chosen of necessity.

To find her…you must let go of all you think you are. To find her…reach to the Stars that heralded your birth with Planets in their fold; making stories new, while tending stories old.

This *Mother* we visit last…for it was she we came to first before we walked upon this Earth as we are now. It was she who cast the colors of our soul's tapestry. It was she who made us rich by the Stars' and Planets' kiss at our birth. And when we die…as Orchil pulls the black thread, taking the body that is hers; Anankê pulls the eight-fold thread of Heavenly blessings unto herself, lifting the soul's colors back through the beltway of the Stars.

We may seek her while we live…to be reminded of our life's promise.

To find her…close your senses to the world around you…and awaken again to the worlds within you. See yourself wrapped in the beautiful colors of Anankê's threads. Among the many colors, you will now see the particular celestial threads that bind the soul to skin…this is the eight-fold thread she weaves.

As before with the black thread of Orchil, pull Anankê's eight-fold thread toward you…pull it down toward Earth and away from its origins in the high Heavens…pull upon the eight-fold thread of Anankê…like a bell pull in a great cathedral…it responds.

Listen... as the Heavens ring and the sirens sing in response to your pulling upon the eight-fold thread of Anankê.

Hold tight upon the eight-fold thread...as your body lifts off the ground and into the sky above...holding fast to her eight-fold thread, you move swiftly away from the Earth and into the vast Heavens, toward the throne of Anankê.

Into Night we journey back...through the veils of velvet black.
Into Night we journey back...through the veils of velvet black.
Into Night we journey back...through the veils of velvet black.

See yourself surrounded by the great velvet black of the Heavens peppered with glittering Stars and turning Planets. Climb beyond Moon, Sun and Stars...rise away...rise above...until even these things seem small beneath you.

See yourself changing from form to formless as you approach the River of Forgetfulness. Be very careful not to drink of its waters...as this is not the death journey; instead move swiftly beyond its gentle currents and back across the hot Plain of Oblivion as a simple soul composed of light and consciousness, pulled along by the eight-fold thread of Anankê.

See now a great pillar of light extending through the Universe. The Heavenly hues of your eight-fold thread find their home within Anankê's great spindle, perched atop this pillar of light.

Rise toward the celestial throne where she sits holding the spindle turning ever between her knees. See also three others, seated at a distance...in witness to all: Lachesis, Clotho, Atropos.

Be still and listen to the songs of the sirens poised purposefully within the Heavens and the whirl of Anankê.

From out of the darkness…beyond the throne of Anankê…
a robed herald of mother and daughters comes. Taking you by
the hand, the herald leads you back under the throne of
Anankê back toward the moments of necessity and choice.

Listen once again to the voice of the herald, "You shall choose
your own deity; that which is necessary for the growth of your
soul will be given to you by Anankê and the Stars and Planets
under her command. The way in which you do this deed, will
be your choice alone. The blessings of virtue will come if you
choose to honor them within the life."

See the herald gather up the tiles of necessity…watch as the
spindle flashes with all the colors of the rainbow and the herald
scatters the tiles upon the ground before you.

Clear your eyes as you gaze down upon the tile closest to your
feet. Look to the glyph…the symbol…whose simplicity encompasses the multiplicity of your natal chart and the whole of this
life's promise. Hold fast to the vision of this tile…let it quicken
all sacred memories within you…remember…. return… to this
moment of perfect clarity.

Now see the herald gather up the tiles of choice. All the
choices…all the patterns of lives are held within the herald's
arms… far more numerous than you imagined before. See all
forms of wealth and poverty….of beauty and ugliness…of
bloodline and ancestry…of strength and weakness. Here great
promise and great error co-exist. Here great understanding
may come to you now.

Watch as the herald scatters the many tiles, upside down, upon
the ground before you…and you walk forward with everything
you possess to choose the pattern of your current life.

Turn over the tile of your choice…read all it indicates in symbol and in script. Hold fast to the vision of this tile…let it quicken all sacred memories within you…remember….return…to this moment of perfect clarity.

And suddenly, with this you….

See Lachesis sends the spirits…chosen,
And Clotho spins the cloth….handwoven,
And Atropos your dewy threads doth seal.

Over pass…and under Throne,
Your soul now journeys down,
Away from Anankê's appeal.

Across the hot Plain of Oblivion,
Beyond the River of Forgetfulness,

Down through the veils of velvet black,
To solid ground, come back, come back.

Down through the veils of velvet black,
To solid ground, come back, come back.

And in this remembrance do seal,
Anankê's bright musing,
And your pattern's choosing,
All of this, your life's ideal.

With each breath in…and each breath out…fan the bellows of your lungs…until you find yourself alive within your waking consciousness…in full possession of all she's given you… Here…Now.

Stillness Meditation

Stillness Method I: Working with the Senses

When we are new to the practice of stillness, we can build our aptitude for this form by working with the natural tendencies of our five senses. During sleep and meditation, our five senses are reoriented toward the inner worlds. As such they form a relationship with our subconscious and the subtle realms.

To begin, imagine your senses are the five petals of a wild rose. When you are engaged in your outer life, your wild rose is wide open with its petals extending outward. To shift your engagement to your inner life, draw in these same extensions, petal by petal, forming the bud of your inward focused consciousness. Far from being a constriction of your senses, this bud-like orientation of your senses opens wide the doors of the inner worlds.

To experiment with this notion, simply close your eyes withdrawing your vision. Take a moment to actually experience this; purposefully take in the world around you, then close your eyes. Notice the dramatic difference between your experience of the world with your eyes open and your eyes closed.

Though it takes a bit more practice, the same dramatic effect is possible with each of the other four senses. If you doubt this, think back to a time when you sat in a meeting and were so absorbed in your own thoughts that you missed several words in the dialog taking place around you. In a moment, someone called your name, suddenly snapping you back into the present moment aware of all you'd missed. All five senses migrate inward and outward all the time.

To start this stillness form, draw inward your sense of sight; again, by simply closing your eyes.

Enfold your sense of hearing, orienting your listening capacity away from the overt sounds around you and toward the still, small voice within you.

Withdraw your sense of touch away from its dense, physical orientation and toward the soft caress of the subtle realms. Become more aware of the subtle majesty of a light breeze, the heat on your skin or the touch of the beings and energies of the inner worlds.

Now, direct your intertwined senses of smell and taste away from the physical world and toward the subtleties of the inner worlds. Let yourself fall open to the soft smells and tastes of your inner world, and the greater inner worlds that enfold you.

With all five senses jointly attuned to the subtle frequencies of the inner worlds, simply sit or lie completely still so that all that moves within is the expansion and contraction of your lungs.

Allow the stillness that comes from the inward direction of your five senses to enfold you...opening you to the wisdom, clarity and peace that lies within the quiet place inside you.

When your time in stillness is complete, simply open the closed bud of your five senses, one by one, orienting each petal and sense back toward the outer world of form.

Stillness Method II: Bone and Breath

A second method for cultivating a meditative stillness relies upon the physical body, versus the extension of the body via the five senses.

For those of us bathed in the nervous system stimulation of computers, cell phones, caffeine and sugar, the body seems to be racing all the time. Thus, it serves our journey into stillness to reconnect with the physical body itself. In Method II, our focus is upon the elements of Earth and Air within us, as bones and breath.

Begin by drawing all of your attention into the deepest physical space within you…where the bones of your body dwell.

Moving beneath the constant firing of the nervous system, muscles and tendons, rekindle your relationship with the "scaffolding" of your physical body.

See and sense your muscles and tendons "hanging" upon the strength of your bones in a loving surrender that releases all physical and mental tension. Simply stay with this image for a few moments. Allowing each passing moment to enable a deeper and deeper trust in the strength of your bones to uphold you.

Focus now on your breath. Engage your sacred imagination so that you can literally see and sense air moving among and around the bones and all they support.

See and sense how the grace of air's flowing movement bathes your inner physical body with the purifying presence of life.

As you continue your deep and rhythmic breathing, allow your muscles and tendons to literally hang upon the strength of your bones while the purifying breath of life circulates, co-creating a peaceful and contemplative space into the center of your being.

Continue this dance between the ever-flowing breath and ever-supportive bones as long as is necessary for you to feel totally and completely still.

When your time in stillness is complete, simply reengage your muscles and tendons...lifting them from the bones and into action again.

Encouraging Words

Many people struggle with stillness, thinking if they can't sit for ten minutes of completely uninterrupted inner silence, they aren't doing it right and thus they give up on stillness altogether.

As an intellectual person with a high metabolism, I had my own struggle learning to cultivate inner stillness. From this experience I encourage you onward by saying this: no matter what happens in your day to day stillness endeavors, don't give up! All your stillness meditations, however successful or unsuccessful, are stored within the cellular memory of your mind and body. If you keep working to build the body's understanding of stillness, suddenly one day, the accumulated body memory of a repeated stillness practice will literally kick in. Then without warning, your whole being will drop, unexpectedly, into a deep, meditative stillness. From that moment onward, stillness will be yours when you seek it.

As with all learned skills, stillness takes practice. Even if you don't notice results, your body is being imprinted with the method and it will, over time, bear fruit. Stillness is one of the many natural states of a human being, thus it is part of who we are. Sometimes we just need a little time and assistance to recover and revive our unused parts.

Endnotes

1. Please note, all elemental and directional associations referenced are Western or Classical in nature and thus akin to the spiritual and magical traditions encompassed within that system. Other systems may have other associations.

2. An aegis is a cape denoting Athena's protection and sponsorship is from highest authority, i.e. Zeus. The aegis was originally a Libyan or Ethiopian women's garment decorated with leather thongs. It signifies her ownership of her own virtue and is worn throughout her maidenhood.

3. Chronicles 1:24 & footnotes in *Oxford Annotated Bible*. The Priestly divisions were ritual work groups in Judaism formed during the reign of King David as documented in Chronicles. In all there were twenty-four divisions. Zadok and Ahimelech were designated by King David to help create the Priestly work groups. Lots were used. Each order was responsible for ministering during a different week and Shabbat, and was stationed as watch at the Tabernacle.

4. The First Hebrew Temple, built by King Solomon, was destroyed in 586 BCE with the Jewish nation exiled to Babylon. After King Cyrus the Great made the reestablishment of Jerusalem and the Temple possible, the Second Temple was built (516 BCE.) Various kings modified the structure. Around 20 CE, King Herod the Great renovated it and thus it became known as Herod's Temple until the Romans destroyed Jerusalem in 70 CE.

5. *The Veneration of the Virgin Mary in the Orthodox Church*. http://www.orthodoxresearchinstitute.org/articles/ dogmatics/dmitri_veneration_mary.htm.

6. Hone, William, *The Lost Books of the Bible*, Random House, 1979.

7. In Aramaic, "nazor" or "nazir" means prince or crown. The Nazoreans were noble descendents of a branch of the royal family of King David. After the conquering of King David's lands during the era of the Maccabees, the royal family retired to a small agricultural town of 150 people, called Nazareth.

8. According to Jacques Baldet, the original word in Genesis so often translated to "sin" actually means "error in judgment." I highly recommend his wonderful book *Jesus the Rabbi Prophet* published by Inner Traditions.

9. Boss, Sarah Jane, editor, *Mary: The Complete Resource*, Oxford University Press, 2007.

10. Wolkstein, Diane and Kramer, Samuel Noah, *Inanna: Queen of Heaven and Earth, Her Stories and Hymns from Sumer,* Harper & Row, New York, 1983.

About the Author

Anastacia J. Nutt is an ordained Minister and Ritualist through *All Seasons Chalice Church/The StarHouse* in Boulder, Colorado where, since 1997, she has co-creatively established several programs of sacred learning including *New Moons for Women, The Path of the Ceremonial Arts for Women, The Path of the Ceremonial Arts for Men* and *Women of Vision* in co-creation with her Priestess partner, Lila Sophia Tresemer. She routinely facilitates public rituals in her home temple and elsewhere.

She is the author of *Unseen Worlds and Practical Aspects of Spiritual Discernment* and *The Sacred Cross: A Transformation Tool for Life*, also available through RJ Stewart Books.

Currently, Anastacia divides her time between the US, UK and Israel where she teaches workshops and offers individual consultations.

Distance learning opportunities include her correspondence course: *Priest & Priestess Arts for the 21st Century* and practical webinars: *The Elements of Spiritual Self-Care, Talismans and Amulets* and *Classical Tarot: Proper Foundations and Applications.*

To inquire about individual or group study, please email her directly at illuminora@yahoo.com.

CPSIA information can be obtained at www.ICGtesting.com
Printed in the USA
BVOW041533110213

312795BV00001BA/6/P

9 780981 924687